An Introduction to the English Writing System

Edinburgh Textbooks on the English Language

Titles in the series include:

An Introduction to English Syntax, 2nd Edition
Jim Miller

An Introduction to International Varieties of English
Laurie Bauer

An Introduction to Middle English
Jeremy Smith and Simon Horobin

An Introduction to Old English, Revised Edition
Richard Hogg, with Rhona Alcorn

An Introduction to Early Modern English
Terttu Nevalainen

An Introduction to English Sociolinguistics
Graeme Trousdale

An Introduction to Late Modern English
Ingrid Tieken-Boon van Ostade

An Introduction to Regional Englishes: Dialect Variation in England
Joan Beal

An Introduction to English Morphology, 2nd Edition
Andrew Carstairs-McCarthy

An Introduction to English Phonology, 2nd Edition
April McMahon

An Introduction to English Semantics and Pragmatics, 3rd Edition
Patrick Griffiths and Christopher Cummins

An Introduction to English Phonetics, 3rd Edition
Richard Ogden

An Introduction to the English Writing System
Marco Condorelli

Visit the Edinburgh Textbooks on the English Language website at
www.edinburghuniversitypress.com/series/ETOTEL

An Introduction to the English Writing System

Marco Condorelli

EDINBURGH
University Press

Edinburgh University Press is one of the leading university presses in the UK. Publishing new research in the arts and humanities, EUP connects people and ideas to inspire creative thinking, open new perspectives and shape the world we live in. For more information, visit www.edinburghuniversitypress.com

Edinburgh University Press Ltd
13 Infirmary Street, Edinburgh EH1 1LT

Typeset in Janson MT
by Cheshire Typesetting Ltd, Cuddington, Cheshire
Printed and bound in the UK using 100% renewable electricity by
CPI Group (UK) Ltd

Cover design: riverdesignbooks.com

A CIP record for this book is available from the British Library

ISBN 978 1 3995 1716 4 (hardback)
ISBN 978 1 3995 1717 1 (paperback)
ISBN 978 1 3995 1718 8 (webready PDF)
ISBN 978 1 3995 1719 5 (epub)

EU Authorised Representative:
Easy Access System Europe
Mustamäe tee 50, 10621 Tallinn, Estonia
gpsr.requests@easproject.com

MIX
Paper | Supporting responsible forestry
FSC® C013604
FSC www.fsc.org

This book is printed using paper from well-managed forests, recycling and other controlled sources

Contents

Figures and tables

Figure

Tables

Foreword

This textbook appears at an interesting time for the study of the English writing system at university. Recent years have seen a surge of interest among scholars and students alike in everything related to English spelling, orthography and literacy. In the not-so-distant past, however, the English writing system was one of the most underrated areas of discussion in English linguistics, due to the fact that writing was considered by earlier generations of researchers as worthy of less empirical attention than speech. A pertinent quote is that of Fred Householder, an American linguist and classical scholar, who once affirmed that "the propositions intuitively felt to be basic by friend and enemy alike [...]", in the American Structuralist School of Linguistics, were that "[...] language is basically speech, and writing is of no theoretical interest" (Householder, 1969: 886). Perhaps also as a result of statements like these, the English writing system has remained a relatively under-researched and undeveloped area of linguistic enquiry for quite a long time. Nevertheless, scholarly contributions from the last couple of decades through to the most recent years have made it possible for a textbook like this to provide a sufficiently complex and informed body of knowledge on the topic.

While English writing system textbooks are rare, there are at least a couple of more recent volumes that align more closely to the aim of the present textbook. Horobin's *A History of English Spelling* (2025), available in the same book series which hosts this book (Edinburgh Textbooks on the English Language), is intended to offer a course in English spelling suitable for an advanced student audience, and provides a complementary title to the present textbook. Horobin's book is divided into two major sections. The first part offers an historical overview of the development of English spelling, from Old English to present-day English. The second section takes a thematic approach on practical aspects of English spelling, considering how changes in the functions, media and attitudes towards the written word have affected the way in which English is spelled. Themes discussed in this second section are those of prescriptivism, gender, proposals for reform, and how to create a spelling-focused research project. Readers who would like to integrate the information provided in the present book with some of the topics mentioned above are encouraged to use Horobin's contribution to the Edinburgh Textbooks on the English Language series.

Another relevant title for this textbook is Cook's *The English Writing System* (2004), which is perhaps less known among fellow writers and readers but is no less valuable. Cook's volume describes issues relating to how people access words on the page, how written English differs from spoken English, which rules give patterns of regularity to English spelling, what punctuation and page layout conventions characterise written English, how children and learners of English as a second language engage with spelling, and what are the similarities and differences in the uses of written English across different geographical locations. Although Cook's book was written with a view of devoting a relatively large teaching space to the subject, and covered extensive ground suitable to both undergraduate and postgraduate students, the English writing system is, to my knowledge, almost never treated as a stand-alone module in English language and linguistics courses today. However, it is a topic that is touched upon, albeit tangentially, across many linguistic subdisciplines, for example phonology and syntax, but also lexicography, the history of English, child language acquisition and sociolinguistics, to mention only some linguistic areas. Outside the remits of linguistics, the English writing system is also a subject of tangential interest to those studying literature, creative writing and publishing, among others.

Given the frequent, inevitable references to topics related to the English writing system in academia today, there is a need for students to have access to a new textbook format and updated contents that will provide them with essential theoretical and practical information on the English writing system, while at the same time being succinct and accessible to non-specialists. The present textbook aims to fulfil this task, describing the English writing system in a way that is functional to a university course where some background knowledge on the topic is expected both theoretically (in preparation for linguistic classes) and practically (in assessments involving disciplines which touch upon the English writing system, whether linguistic or extra-linguistic). Thus, the present textbook may be used in tandem with Horobin's textbook, and it is recommended that it is studied ahead of Horobin's contribution in order to acquire essential theoretical and background knowledge on the subject.

Writing, and all of the principles and rules surrounding it, is the primary means of communication through which most linguistic disciplines are studied and by which examples of linguistic features and processes are given. Yet, despite the importance of the subject in the linguistics of English, some of the most basic information on the topic still remains unknown to or misunderstood by many. A widespread problem among students today, which may be the result of the fact that the subject is not studied sufficiently at university, is their inability to see spelling forms, from within the confines of the linguistic modules touching upon the English writing system, as subjects of interest that enable one to think critically about the socio-pragmatic implications of writing. A better understanding of the functioning and structuring of the English writing system will help students to use terminology correctly and rigorously when focusing specifically on the study of elements in the English writing system. Moreover, it will enable them to think more proactively about connections between written English and all other facets of the language, as well as connections between linguistic and extra-linguistic subjects.

In order to help students with attaining these objectives, three different steps are followed in this textbook, each corresponding respectively to a different book section. The first part of this textbook (Part I), titled 'Context', attempts to act as a first reference point for those interested in learning, more or less from scratch, about the English writing system. This section offers a connection to issues involving phonology, morphology and semantics, thus appealing to a wide readership among students of linguistics. The discussion is divided into three individual chapters. Chapter 1 offers an introduction to the main features of speech and writing as two different but complementary modes of communication. The purpose of this chapter is to help students to understand that studying the English writing system inevitably entails focusing on specific aspects of communication, which may be distinct from those of speech.

Chapter 2 provides an overview of writing system typology and summarises some of the most relevant research conducted over the last four decades in order to understand the place of the English writing system in the existing typological framework of writing systems. Chapter 3 delves deeper into some of the issues covered in the research material surveyed in the previous chapter, offering a description of the principles underlying English spelling (as proposed in the existing literature) and a discussion about how these principles influence our understanding of the English writing system as a complex communicative framework. While this chapter is more theoretical in nature, it still has a marked literature review orientation, and acts as a bridge between this first part and the second part of the textbook.

The second section of this textbook (Part II), titled 'Elements', has a more theoretical tone, as it provides definitions for some of the most frequently found key terms in writing system research and their relevance to the English writing system. The first chapter in Part II, Chapter 4, offers a detailed discussion of key terminology used to understand the English writing system ('orthography', 'script' and 'spelling'), expanding on some of the labels discussed in this introductory section (see below). The chapter also provides a discussion of the connection between the English writing system and grapholinguistics, a branch of writing-related knowledge stemming primarily from German scholarly endeavours. Theoretical work in grapholinguistics has contributed to strengthening our definitions of key elements in the English writing system, in a way that integrates, rather than contradicts, contributions to knowledge made by scholars specialising in the English writing system. Drawing on definitions existing in grapholinguistics, this chapter describes the function and role of the graph, the glyph and the grapheme, the building blocks of English spelling. Chapters 5 and 6 are quite similar to each other in terms of structure, and focus on selected elements in the English writing system. These are, respectively, punctuation and capitalisation, which, as part of their many roles, also complement grammatical, lexical and semantic features in English. Therefore, this section is also likely to appeal mostly, but not only, to linguists.

The third and last part of the textbook (Part III), titled 'Connections', focuses on interdisciplinary links between the English writing system on one hand, and sociology, bibliography, the psychology of reading and literacy studies on the other hand. While the previous two sections of the textbook have focused on topics exclusively linguistic in nature, the purpose of this section is to encourage readers to think about the English writing system as an area also embracing extra-linguistic subjects. Those approaching this section should not expect a comprehensive coverage of all potential links existing between the English writing system and all relevant extra-linguistic disciplines, as attempting to achieve this task would require a much more extensive scope than that allowed in a textbook. Rather, what readers can take from this section is a range of extra-linguistic examples that are most relevant to those interested in topics involving standardisation, the printing press and literacy acquisition. These are some of the empirical areas frequently connected to research in English orthography today, and topics in which I, as author of this textbook, have working experience.

The first chapter in Part III (Chapter 7) focuses on the social meaning behind variation and standardisation in English orthography, arguing that orthography is a valuable signal of cultural, historical and social identity. The second part of the chapter discusses the relevance of bibliography and book history in the study of English orthography, explaining how these areas of academic enquiry complement sociological research in the English writing system. The discussion focuses on bibliographic aspects of particular interest to those wishing to study English orthography from a diachronic perspective, and especially the analysis of paper and printing type. Chapter 8 continues the discussion about the correlation between the English writing system and interdisciplinary areas, focusing on the psychology of reading and literacy studies. The chapter begins by highlighting some of the ways in which book history and the psychology of reading are both complementary and different, and explores some case studies in word recognition and text comprehension where English orthography plays an important part. The second part of the chapter explains the close correlation between the psychology of reading and literacy studies, reporting on noteworthy case studies in the acquisition of reading and writing skills where English orthography holds a key role. The final chapter in Part Three, Chapter 9, provides a brief conclusion that reflects on this textbook's overall contribution and its limitations, and offers some suggestions for future work in the English writing system.

Although this textbook assumes minimal knowledge of linguistics, definitions relating to elements in the English writing system (and other key linguistic definitions such as those involving the phoneme and the morpheme) are given upon first mention. The textbook also features a glossary, which reiterates some of the most important definitions for the study of the English writing system given throughout the chapters, as well as a number of exercises, which encourage readers to consolidate knowledge by providing definitions of key terms in their own words and by reflecting about some of the points made in each chapter. All individual chapters, with the exception of the concluding one, also provide suggestions for further reading, which give an opportunity for readers to extend their knowledge of specific theoretical definitions or pragmatic aspects of the English writing system, as discussed in this textbook. With that said, a number of important keywords for the study of the English writing system ought to be explained now in order to facilitate readers' understanding of this textbook, though definitions will be expanded on across the textbook, when needed. The keywords in question are 'spelling', 'orthography', 'writing system' and 'script'.

While 'spelling' and 'orthography' are frequently used interchangeably in popular discourse, the two terms are characterised by nuanced differences in linguistics. The linguistic understanding of *spelling* is that of the individual letters that form a word, whereas *orthography* includes not only spelling but also additional components of the English writing system, including punctuation, capitalisation, emphasis (for example, italics), word boundaries and diacritics (for instance, accents) (Coulmas, 1996a: 379–380, 477; Condorelli and Rutkowska, 2023: 3). Thus, for example, the spelling of the word 'Naïve' is <n>,[1] <a>, <i>, <v> and <e>, but the orthographic version of this same word includes a capital <N> and a diaeresis over the letter <i>, as in <ï>. The term 'orthography' is sometimes also used to indicate the set of conventions followed as standard in order to allow written English to work as a system. As will be explained in Chapter 7, these conventions have undergone a process of standardisation in the past, so that, today, written English generally exhibits less variation than spoken English.

While this second definition of 'orthography' may potentially blur that of 'writing system', the expression *writing system* should be intended as a more generic term indicating the overall visual apparatus used to write down a language; *orthography*, instead, is to be seen as a more specific set of principles applied to said apparatus for it to function as an instrument of communication (Baker, 1997: 93). Another commonly used term that could cause some confusion is that of 'script', which, in informal discourse, may be mistaken for 'writing system', 'spelling' or 'orthography'. In linguistics, the term *script* refers to the pragmatic set of symbols used in a writing system of a given language; for English, these are the letters from the Roman alphabet (*a*, *b*, *c*, and so on), which are also available in other writing systems in the world (e.g. Italian, Spanish, German, and so on) (Coulmas, 1996a: 454). In this sense, different writing systems may draw on the same script in order to represent individual written units (Gnanadesikan, 2023: 30). In this textbook, references to all four different layers of understanding of written English (spelling, orthography, writing system and script) will be made, although not necessarily always explicitly. However, descriptions of English spelling and orthography will be more prominent in this textbook, as these are major theoretical and functional areas of the English writing system, and therefore lend themselves to more in-depth educational discussions (see Condorelli and Voeste, 2020: 248).

One last point that needs to be addressed in the introductory part of this textbook is that of the chronological scope followed in this book, which is primarily focused on present-day linguistic issues, though the

[1] Angle brackets are a widely accepted convention for indicating spelling/orthographic units, and they are used in this book for the same purpose.

discussion also makes several references to historical topics. Like many other areas in English linguistics, the English writing system can be studied both from an historical and from a present-day perspective. The historical perspective deals with the past, while the present-day perspective is focused on present-day features and uses of the English writing system.

A widely discussed topic in connection to the history of English spelling is, for example, how some word spellings in sixteenth-century English were coined in an attempt to recreate a connection with their original Latin and French etymons (see, for example, Scragg, 1974: 52–54; Brengelman, 1980: 346; Görlach, 1991: 56–57; Salmon, 1999: 21; Nevalainen, 2006: 32; Upward and Davidson, 2011: 190–192; Horobin, 2013: 111–113; Rutkowska, 2013: 217–248; Condorelli, 2022: 171–191). Many of the word spellings forged at the time following this rationale found a permanent place in English writing practice and still exist today. Thus, for example, the spelling of the word *debt*, which appeared as *dette* in Middle English, was revised following Latin *debitum*; *doubt*, spelled as *doute(n)* in Middle English, was changed following Latin *dubitare*; *indict*, spelled as *endite(n)* in Middle English, was modified according to Latin **indictare*; and *victuals*, appearing as *vitailes* in Middle English, was amended following Latin *victualia* (examples from Nevalainen, 2006: 32).

The present-day approach to studying the English writing system covers relatively permanent aspects of structure and function of English writing today (Carney, 1994: 3–4). This approach frequently concerns itself with establishing a systematic understanding of both the writer's/reader's and the speaker's/hearer's experiences of written English, exploring how the English writing system is applied to produce and to understand language in everyday situations. The present-day approach generally allows for a more descriptive perspective on the English writing system, rather than an explicatory one, which is more typical of the historical approach (Carney, 1994: 3). Cook's *The English Writing System*, for example, describes the inner workings of present-day English orthography to show that functionality is paramount for allowing the English writing system to be usable and intelligible in our society.

The historical and the present-day approaches to discussing the English writing system are not necessarily in opposition. As argued by Carney (1994: 3), both perspectives together allow for a more complete understanding of the way in which the English writing system works, and the reasons why English orthography operates the way that it does. The reason why this textbook largely departs from a discussion of the synchronic side of the English writing system is chiefly practical:

students approaching the history of English spelling first need to be acquainted with the basics of the English writing system as a theoretical and pragmatic framework, before attempting to understand how and where specific principles and processes originated. At the same time, however, it is hoped that the historical perspectives given across several later chapters in this book (especially Chapters 5 to 8), which focus mostly on the sixteenth and the seventeenth centuries, following my area of expertise, will allow students to view the study of the English writing system not as a topic that involves learning a set of dry, unexplainable rules, but rather as an object of principled reasoning which has gone through times of experimentation and rationalisation.

Acknowledgements

The writing of this textbook has taken a long time, as several life events have taken place throughout its development, from its earliest stages to its final draft. This project has also presented several intellectual challenges, which stemmed from combining old and new information in what is a growing, yet relatively new area of knowledge. Several colleagues have assisted in overcoming the challenges mentioned above and letting this project see the light of day, easing the burden of what feels like one of the most difficult projects that I have worked on so far. Many thanks are owed to Heinz Giegerich and Bettelou Los, editors of the Edinburgh Textbooks on the English Language series, Laura Quinn, commissioning editor at Edinburgh University Press, and Helena Heald, who covered Laura's position during her leave. I also have a great deal of appreciation for my anonymous peer reviewers, who have shared precious comments at various stages of this project. My greatest debt of gratitude is owed to Isobel Clements, for letting me run the final stretch of this project in my spare time, while being in receipt of an Early Career Fellowship from the Leverhulme Trust. I also thank the Leverhulme Trust for sponsoring part of this project, namely the sections connected to and stemming from my current research.

Part I

Context

1 Modes of communication

1.1 Focus of this section

This textbook is about the English writing system, a communicative framework operating within the remits of the English language. The overall aim of this first section of the book (Part I), titled 'Context', is that of equipping students embarking on a study of the English writing system with essential background, introductory information on the topic. In particular, this first section pursues the threefold goal of discussing how speech and writing are different from each other; describing the various types of writing systems existing in the world; and, through the identification of principles regulating English spelling, identifying the place of the English writing system in the intricate mosaic of the world's writing systems. The approach used to address these three points is that of providing an updated literature review that summarises key points in a way that is, it is hoped, easy to access, in terms of language and contents, for university students who approach the subject of this textbook as part of a broader linguistic syllabus.

The purpose of this first chapter in particular is that of reflecting on some of the most remarkable features distinguishing speech from writing, as two modes of communication with their own individual forms (internal organisations) and functions (purposes). Although communicative forms and functions are usually taken for granted when focusing on the study of the English writing system, acquiring greater awareness of the differences existing between speech and writing is, for a student of linguistics, a useful starting point to understanding the complex relationship between the two. Focusing on a systematic description of communicative linguistic frameworks in only one of the two levels of communication inevitably entails, for the student of linguistics, analysing a smaller portion of linguistic knowledge, while also appreciating the complex nature of human communication and all the historical, cultural and functional peculiarities underlying it. To begin our discussion about these inherent peculiarities, let us briefly depart from a little anecdote on ancient Greek culture as an example, which tells us about the high value that the Greeks bestowed on writing due to its intrinsic communicative functions.

According to an ancient Greek myth, Prometheus, a titan living on Mount Olympus, defied all the other Olympian gods by stealing fire from them and gifting it to humans in the guise of technology, wisdom and civilisation. In some variants of the ancient Greek myth, Prometheus also passed on to humans intellectual abilities that were once possessed only by the immortal gods, including those of doing mathematics and agriculture, practising medicine, experimenting with science and writing (Suddendorf, 2013: 103). While writing has a socio-historical, cultural and cognitive origin rather than a mythological one, Greek mythology reminds us of the importance of writing in our history and gives us a glimpse into the status of writing as an intellectual ability in ancient Greek culture. Ranked alongside disciplines such as mathematics, agriculture, medicine and science, writing was perceived in antiquity as a superlative, godly ability that elevated those who possessed it from all the mortals who were 'only' able to speak in order to communicate.

The contrast between writing as an 'immortal' and speech as a 'mortal' skill is an analogy that reflects the function that both modes of communication had in the development of ancient history. Writing was for permanent communication; speech was for temporary linguistic transactions. Of course, writing also had ephemeral purposes, for example when it was used on wax tablets for taking personal notes, but these uses were less frequent in ancient times than they are now, due to the scarce availability of primary resources and the limited number of individuals who were able to write. For the most part, writing allowed the ancient Greeks – and indeed most historical civilisations – to transmit to their future generations the fruit of cultural, political, mathematical and literary achievements. Speech, instead, was at the heart of socio-political activities, religious ceremonies and, despite its increasingly difficult relationship with writing, also the art of rhetoric (Schloemann, 2002: 133–146).

The dynamics of writing and speech in ancient Greece are somewhat different from those that characterise our modern society, not least because our levels of literacy today are much different than those of the far past. Still, a degree of similarity may be found, as our contemporary world, in all its cultural, political and educational facets, builds upon the shoulders of our ancient ancestors and the early civilisations which roamed our planet. Today, our communicative experience as social beings embedded in complex societal systems normally unfolds following what Finnegan (2024: 248) calls a 'multimodal' process. The way in which we communicate is complex because it follows multiple layers unfolding all at the same time, frequently without us realising it, and all the nuances involved in these many layers of communication are needed for communication to be effective (Finnegan, 2024: 248). Our abilities to speak and write not only work as the foundation of multimodality, but also closely interact with our capacity to hear, see, taste, smell and touch. Interaction across all five of our senses occurs, for example, when communication is initiated with a little physical nudge or a handshake and is followed up by speech, or when a schoolteacher delivers a lesson orally while also using hand gestures, and writing down words on the blackboard (see Finnegan, 2024: 44–45).

One of the reasons why multimodal communication occurs in our society is that of ensuring that information is delivered correctly and effectively. In some of the more sophisticated restaurants, for example, a waiter orally offers guests details on the drinks and the range of food available while they hand over a printed copy of the menu. The availability of multimodal means of communication also allows individuals who are less proficient in one of the two modes of communication, for example writing, to compensate for their linguistic deficiency by relying on the other mode as a way of filling in any gaps left in their understanding. A neat example is that involving individuals who have learned a language from their mother (a native speaker) and were never taught how to read it (for more details, see Finnegan, 2024: 248).

In most languages and contexts, speech and writing have complementary roles in our multimodal communication by virtue of their inherent individual properties, which might be generalised as follows. Speech is temporary, often unprompted, and provides a more immediate connection, at least in everyone's perception, between one's thoughts and the act of expressing them to the world (Cook, 2004: 33). Writing, instead, usually lasts longer than speech, generally undergoes a degree of planning, and represents a slower, less immediate connection between one's thoughts and the same expressive act (Cook, 2004: 33). The ways in which speaking and writing are produced, which will be better described in section 1.2 below, entail the fact that the former propagates over time and the latter extends across space (Meletis and Dürscheid, 2022: 24–25). Both speech and writing have structural elaboration and complexity, which makes them most apt to represent language, of which the human faculty of both are active components. While readers of this textbook will likely be familiar with the linguistic definition of 'language', it is important to provide a quick reference to it here in order to better illustrate how speech and writing operate in it.

Language is defined as a cognitive faculty that gives us the ability to communicate with others (Rogers, 2005: 2). According to Hazen (2015: 3–4),

> Language is the discrete combinatorial system humans use most for communication. *Discrete* means 'separate' here, and *combinatorial* means 'ability to add together.' We take small separate parts, push them together in specific combinations, and create larger parts of language. For spoken languages, we store collections of sounds together with their associated ideas. We call them words, and they can be short (e.g. *I*) or long (e.g. *Mississippi*), but they are all sets of sounds connected to a meaning. With those words, we build larger phrases such as noun phrases (e.g. *most squids*), verb phrases (e.g. *crushed the daisies*), and prepositional phrases (e.g. *on the kangaroo*).

As one can gather from Hazen's quote, language is an abstract communicative system consisting of various linguistic levels (e.g. phonology, morphology, syntax, lexicography, semantics and pragmatics). These linguistic levels ultimately co-operate by allowing our brain to exchange information with that of other individuals of our species who speak the same language, usually following a more or less standardised format which can be easily produced and understood. Successful exchange of information occurs by means of two principal linguistic properties, which make communication possible on an interpersonal level, and which are intrinsic features of both speech and writing: meaning and structure. *Meaning* is defined by Hazen (2015: 19) in a way that adds further to our understanding of language as described above:

> Meaning is the goal for language and for all forms of communication. To communicate is to mean something. For humans, many different ways to convey meaning are used every day. If two people approach a doorway at the same time, and one pauses, the other person might take that pause to mean "permission to go first." Language is a subset of human communication, but it is a special subset. As far as linguists know, the ability to acquire and use language is a genetically endowed, species-specific trait. Only humans do it. In the evolution of this ability, meaning must have been one of the first components, since we find meaning to be part of all animal communication systems.

Structure, instead, is the way in which language organises "the bricks and mortar used to build language" (Hazen, 2015: 22), in a format which is, in principle, predictable, understandable and reproducible by all human beings. Both meaning and structure are regulated linguistic properties that depend heavily on *vocabulary*, the set of words available in language, and *grammar*, the group of rules which regulate the creation of clauses, phrases and words. Since meaning and structure are intrinsic to both speech and writing, vocabulary and grammar are transmitted to both modes of communication, albeit in different modalities. In the case of speech, meaning is created by piecing together individual sounds in order to form words, which in turn operate according to grammatical rules. In writing, instead, meaning occurs by putting together graphic units that, individually or in combination, represent words, and by distinguishing individual words by means of blank spaces. Thus, while speech and writing operate following the same underlying linguistic mechanisms, the ways in which these are realised by language users are different. Additional comparative insights along these lines are provided in sections 1.2 and 1.3 below.

1.2 Speech and writing in comparison

The physical characteristics of the acts of speaking and writing are at the heart of the operational differences existing between these two modes of communication. In order to help readers to spell out these otherwise intuitively known differences, a more in-depth description of the physical mechanisms underlying speech and writing is warranted. With speech, muscles in the mouth (including the tongue) and the face are called into action; the lungs, responsible for creating the airflow, or interrupting it, are also involved in the process (Cook, 2004: 32). Communicating through writing, instead, involves relying on different muscles than those normally used for the production of speech. In the act of writing, understood in its traditional sense, hand motion is required, often in coordination with even more precise, nuanced movements of the fingers, depending on whether one is holding a pen, and whether this occurs with the right or the left hand, or whether typing is involved (Cook, 2004: 32). Ultimately, the brain is responsible for coordinating all muscular movements involved in both modes of communication, whether they are those of the face or the hand. However, the amount of energy required for either writing or speaking is different, as are the levels of concentration needed to ensure coordination and to absorb information.

Processing the meaning of a spoken sentence traditionally involves perceiving sound frequencies through the eardrum, inside one's ear, and deciphering these sounds into distinguishable chunks of meaning. Processing the meaning of a written sentence, instead, involves using sight to interpret the visual information that is left by the writer on the material they write on, whether it is a piece of paper or a tablet display screen. Impairments in the ability to hear or see, when the hearing or sight organs are damaged, mean that the process of absorbing written information will have to occur somewhat differently than the traditional ways followed by most. For the hearing impaired, for example, it will involve the use of more visual cues, whether these are captured reading sign language or following lip movements more closely. For the sight impaired, taking in information will involve the use of touch-based cues, whether these consist of 'feeling' the environment surrounding them in order to explore the world or whether they involve using Braille, which can be read either on embossed paper or by using refreshable Braille displays that connect to computers and smartphone devices.

An important point made briefly in section 1.1, which stems directly from the argument made here about the mechanical differences existing between speaking and writing (and which therefore warrants further elaboration in this new light), is that of the durability of the two modes of communication: speaking is more transient while writing is more permanent. Speech is, as argued in Cook (2004: 33), severely constrained by the ephemeral nature of the event. The faculty of speaking is inevitably bound to our bodily nature and, therefore, it perishes with us at the end of our lifetime (Meletis and Dürscheid, 2022: 21). There are also physical limitations in the act of speaking. When we speak, our message passes on to the interlocutor if it is sufficiently loud and if the person we are talking to is close enough to perceive the sound waves produced by our vocal cords.

While our present-day technology enables us to record speech in the form of audio files, podcasts and tape recorders, the way in which the recordings must be played back to hear the words again makes recorded speech remarkably different from written records (Meletis and Dürscheid, 2022: 23). When played back, the recordings always follow the unidirectional arrow of time to which default speech is bound, and the words are lost once the recording ends. If one plays back the recording on repeat, individual sounds, and the words represented by them, are still lost as soon as they are produced, but the continued reproduction of the whole string is one of "transient permanence" (Meletis and Dürscheid, 2022: 23).

In any case, the aid of present-day technology in the iteration of speech only applies to our day and age. With the exception of comparatively few examples from the last few decades, all of the spoken utterances produced in the history of humanity are lost, with the consequence that our understanding of historical spoken English is hampered by the scant evidence (mostly indirect, such as that of reported speech in trial documents or literary rhymes) surviving to this day. Even for historical periods where there is relatively more evidence available, as for the centuries closer to our contemporary age, our knowledge of speech is selective and most likely distorted.

The durability of writing, instead, is owed to the fact that this mode of communication usually depends on materials external to our body (Meletis and Dürscheid, 2022: 20). If writing is left on a durable surface, the message sometimes outlives us and passes on to someone else's attention without it needing us to be present to facilitate the process. Through this materially facilitated relay system, examples of English language as it was used in the past have come to us today. The marks etched on the Ruthwell Cross, for example, a well-known Anglo-Saxon sculpture, echo the words inhabiting the minds of the people responsible for carving the message in the eighth century AD. The words are as follows: ᛣᚱᛁᛋᛏ ᚹᚫᛋ ᚩᚾ ᚱᚩᛞᛁ ᚻᚹᛖᚦᚱᚫ / ᚦᛖᚱ ᚠᚢᛋᚫ ᚠᛠᚱᚱᚪᚾ ᛤᚹᚩᛗᚢ / ᚫᚦᚦᛁᛚᚫ ᛏᛁᛚ ᚪᚾᚢᛗ / ᛁᚳ ᚦᚫᛏ ᚪᛚ ᛒᛁᚻ, which can be transcribed as *Krist wæs on rodi. Hweþræ / þer fusæ fearran kwomu / æþþilæ til anum / ic þæt al bih[eald]*, and translated into 'Christ was on the cross, and there hastening from far came they to the noble prince. I beheld all that' (Browne, 1897: 245). Through these written words, individuals from Anglo-Saxon England are able to communicate with us today, and will carry on communicating to future generations of readers as long as the stone survives the test of time.

Besides the point made about durability, additional physical differences may be noticed between writing and speech. In particular, writing can be planned and, depending on the purpose of the written message, it may undergo several drafts before a final written message is conveyed more formally (Cook, 2004: 34–35). Unlike writing, speech cannot be manipulated once it has been produced because sounds cannot be retrieved once they are out of our lungs and they disperse in the air. Although it is possible to edit a statement by uttering a follow-up sentence, this action is not equivalent to fully erasing the sentence and rewriting a new one as a replacement before anyone can read it (Cook, 2004: 34–35).

Since speech and writing are two distinct physical events, each of them transmits different levels of information. One of the peculiarities of speaking is that of conveying voice tone, which fluctuates in order to indicate different sentence types (a question, a statement, an exclamation, a hesitation) (Cook, 2004: 37). This type of information is also supplemented by additional acoustic nuances such as pauses and fluency, which give us a sense of the speaker's state of mind – for example, whether the speaker feels nervous or at ease. Similarly, stress is sometimes used during speech to help the listener to distinguish different parts of a sentence or to disambiguate two very similar words (e.g. in American English, 'I mean past-*or* not past-*ah*') (Cook, 2004: 37).

A way in which written communication tries to convey some of the nuances available in speech is through fonts, punctuation and syntax. By **bolding**, <u>underlining</u> or *italicising* a word, for example, a written sentence may convey the sense of urgency that an uttered statement might carry (e.g. 'do not *lose* that pen, okay?') (Cook, 2004: 37). Likewise, spoken questions or exclamations can be pinpointed using question and exclamation marks, while hesitations can be signalled using ellipses (e.g. 'I'm not sure what to say, but …') (see Chapter 5, section 5.1). Parallel examples involving manipulation of syntax for expressive purposes include word repetition (e.g. 'That was a wise idea, a very wise idea'), syntactic arrangement (e.g. 'Little did Mark know that it was him who knew the whole story') and sentence fragmentation (e.g. 'Guess what? I'm engaged!') (Meletis and Dürscheid, 2022: 23–24).

Because they unfold over time, the thoughts underlying speech are usually produced spontaneously and with the appropriate degree of detail needed as the spoken sentence is being uttered. In particular, since speech is usually produced in a context that allows for a dialogic interaction with the hearer, it is normally devoid of the extensive descriptive elements that writing may otherwise have (Cook, 2004: 35–36). Examples include 'She's Mark's mother', uttered while pointing to a lady standing outside the supermarket, or 'He's been teaching English in high school for five years', spoken while referring to a young man that a couple have just met. Sometimes, the scarcity of contextual material in spoken utterances helps the speaker to split down complex thoughts into simple sentences, so that the words uttered can be stored in the hearer's memory while new sentences are produced during the course of a conversation. As a result of the act of quickly producing an utterance with little detail, speech might have structural and lexical imprecision, hesitations and contradictions (Cook, 2004: 34).

Unlike speech, writing is, by default, monologic, which means that the reader does not usually engage in an interactive conversation with the writer.[1] For this reason, the writer has to ensure that sufficient

[1] Although writing is primarily monologic, there are examples of written communication that are, admittedly, more dialogic in nature, as with letter correspondence and chat conversation. Speech may also occur monologically, as with university lectures, press conferences and church sermons, but even in these contexts it generally follows the patterns illustrated above, to allow audiences to process meaning efficiently (Meletis and Dürscheid, 2022: 22).

information is conveyed in writing to allow the reader to understand the written message without the need to ask for further details (Meletis and Dürscheid, 2022: 22). Returning to the examples made in the paragraph above, the sentences in quotation marks, which represent speech, would include, if they were to be reported in writing, all the additional descriptive information provided in the same examples above (i.e. *pointing to a lady standing outside the supermarket* and *referring to the young man that a couple have just met*). Likewise, spoken words that convey timing or spatial information, like *yesterday*, *tomorrow*, *today*, *in an hour*, *in six months* but also *here*, *there* and *yonder*, would have little meaning in writing without context. For these words to have meaningful deictic values, they would have to be supplemented with some reference material at some point in the text, or to be embedded in direct speech, to allow the reader to navigate time and space effectively (see Cook, 2004: 35–36 for additional examples).

Deictic elements available in writing that do not require the strategies described above are often those that are not time-sensitive (e.g. *first*, *subsequently*, *meanwhile*) and allow the reader to return to a previous passage if any information is missed during a first reading. In this context, a writer may also use expressions like *the former* and *the latter* for the sake of brevity, while a speaker is normally more inclined to repeat explicitly nouns or actions for simplicity and clarity (Cook, 2004: 35–36). Likewise, writing may feature elliptic grammar, where the verb *to be*, otherwise expected in speech, is omitted, for example in announcements such as 'strong winds across the south-east of England' or 'queues ahead'. Other comparable examples include written sentences where different tenses are used from those normally expected in speech, such as in the following newspaper lines: 'recycled material likely leading to a reduction of CO2 in the atmosphere', 'no trains heading to Edinburgh this weekend due to a national strike' and '45-year-old arrested for burglary'. Some additional abbreviation examples in writing include the use of forms like *approx.* and *c.*, which instead are always pronounced fully in speech ('approximately' and 'circa') (see Cook, 2004: 39–43).

Differences between speech and writing of the type examined here have been measured systematically. Results from a study conducted by Leech et al. (2001, as reported in Cook, 2004: 41), which surveyed 100 million words from the British National Corpus, complement some of the insights into the lexical differences between speech and writing mentioned above. Written English, the authors argue, has a much larger proportion of common nouns, general adjectives, articles (especially *the*), singular proper nouns (e.g. *London*) and the preposition *of*. Spoken English, instead, has a higher frequency of personal pronouns (*I*, *it*, *you*) and frequent verbs like *take.* In addition, written language is more prone to containing low-frequency words, which contribute to creating a sense of sophistication and complexity. To use Halliday's examples, while spoken English frequently features words such as *thing, people, way, do, make, get, have, go, good, many,* written English is more likely to present words such as *organisms, semantics* and *propagate,* which are rarer in everyday speech (Halliday, 1989: 64–65). The way in which the type and frequency of individual words and their arrangement in sentence contexts vary between speech and writing is regulated by some of the dialogic and monologic purposes intrinsic to the two modes of communication described earlier.

1.3 Uses and functions

The previous section has made reference to some of the linguistic properties distinguishing speech from writing as two mutually interactive linguistic levels. Examples of the linguistic types illustrated at the end of section 1.2 in particular alert us to the complexities underlying language production in speech and writing, in light of the purposes that each of them plays in the intricate cognitive process that is language. Within their respective purposes, speech and writing have a variety of *uses,* depending on context and our innate cognitive behaviour. Speech, for example, may be used for eliciting laughter (as in the case of a stand-up comedy show) or to reprehend somebody (for example, a teaching telling off a student). Writing, instead, may be used to record one's own train of thoughts (for example, in a personal diary) and for verifying academic abilities (for example, a university written exam).

Within each of the examples above, there are variations defined by individual preferences, which may change according to personality, education level and language use abilities. There are also linguistic fluctuations deriving from dialectal variation and register. As sociolinguistics and dialectology have demonstrated, variation in speech exists in ways that are socially based, in terms of region, class, gender and/or generation. Register variation is owed to the variety of English that is used in specific contexts, driven by a number of variables such as the individuals involved and the purpose for which spoken or written English is used (for example, formal, informal, technical and colloquial registers) (Halliday, 1989: 42).

A helpful way of grouping together different uses of speech and writing, which complements the distinction made so far between dialogic and monologic purposes, may be found in the contrast established by Brown and Yule (1983: 12) between the *transactional function,* typically fulfilled by writing, and the *interactional function*, traditionally fulfilled by speech. The transactional function consists in the act of transmitting information, whether it is an event that happened in the past, a scenario occurring at present, or the intention of doing something in the future (Brown and Yule, 1983: 11). The interactional function, instead, consists in connecting human beings with one another for specific purposes, mostly social in nature (Brown and Yule, 1983: 11). The main purpose of the transactional function of writing is that of making sure that information is transferred accurately (e.g. a letter from the school principal). The main purpose of the interactional function of speaking, instead, is that of ensuring that the intended social communicative exchange occurs successfully (e.g. in 'Did you have a good day?').

While those above may be considered general trends, there are of course also exceptions where speech takes on a transactional function and writing has an interactional function. When speech has transactional value, this is usually with the purpose of achieving or obtaining something practical in a real-life situation. Example scenarios include that of a cashier announcing the total amount a lady owes for her groceries, a patient telling his doctor what his symptoms are and asking for medication to address them, and a customer complaining about a wrong order to the restaurant manager. Birthday-wishes letters and tourist postcards are examples of interactional writing, while a student's face-to-face appointment with a professor might begin with casual greetings (interaction) and then proceed to the professor answering the student's question about an upcoming assignment (transaction) (Brown and Yule, 1983: 11).

Overall, the lesson given by the points covered so far is simple but important for successfully embarking on a study of the English writing system. Written English should not just be intended as a transcription of spoken conversation, and speech is not to be taken as a framework to dictate what written English should look like (Halliday, 1989: 41). Complexities underlying speech and writing go beyond the patterns that we can easily see on the surface. While the lexical and grammatical examples discussed in section 1.2 may offer some obvious examples, there are also profound historical reasons underlying the discrepancies between the two modes of communication, which may not be as self-apparent. Between the fifteenth and the eighteenth centuries in particular, for example, English underwent a series of sound changes that affected Middle English long vowels, thus causing a mismatch between what were becoming fixed word spellings through the input of the printing press and the way these word spellings were being pronounced. Because of the Great Vowel Shift, words like *meet* and *see* changed in pronunciation from Middle English /meːt/ and /seː/ to Early Modern English /miːt/ and /siː/ (Nevalainen, 2006: 7).

The changes affecting individual words frequently transcended the simple shift from pronunciation 'A' to pronunciation 'B', and rather underwent myriad different pronunciations, creating a pot-pourri of complex sound-to-spelling correlations. The Great Vowel Shift, Nevalainen indicates (2006: 120), was a concatenation of small, localised changes rather than a unique, easily identifiable movement towards Received Pronunciation. These large-scale changes were probably caused by the massive migration occurring from the east and central Midlands to the south of England from the mid-fourteenth century onwards in the wake of the developing wool trade. While the migrants brought with them a variety of dialects, Londoners likely changed their own vowel system in order to distinguish themselves from the new settlers, triggering another wave of sound-to-spelling mismatches (however, see Minkova, 2014: 235–236 for an argument about the complexities underlying the task of verifying these issues).

Historical processes like the phonological one explained above have fuelled the popular assumption that speech is "disorganised, fragmentary and simple" while writing is "highly organised, structured and complex" (Halliday, 1989: 87). The perception is that speech is more easily subjected to unexpected, radical and highly noticeable changes, and therefore must be regulated, one may wrongly assume, by looser rules than those underlying writing. In reality, both speech and writing are systematically and rigorously organised, albeit each in their own way. The structural features discussed in this chapter for writing in particular can usually be recognised without them being openly acknowledged as done especially in section 1.2. A passage given by Halliday (1989: 87) from Toulmin's philosophical book titled *Human Understanding* (1972: 175–176) is as good an example as any other:

> We have defined the content of a scientific discipline by reference to three interrelated sets of elements: (1) the current explanatory goals of the science, (2) its current repertory of concepts and explanatory procedures, (3) the accumulated experience of the scientists working in this particular discipline – i.e., the outcome of their efforts to fulfil their current explanatory ambitions, by applying the valuable repertory of concepts and explanation procedures.

In most cases, the level of intuitive understanding that can be gained from examples like that provided above is sufficient for embarking on a study of the English writing system. A fuller awareness of the differences between speech and writing, however, as offered in this chapter, enriches our understanding of the communicative world in which writing system theory operates, and illuminates ways in which the information gained from the remaining part of this textbook applies in each reader's academic pathway.

Discussion Material

1. Provide short definitions of *speech*, *writing* and *language*, using words that are different from those available in this chapter. Note that more than one definition may be given for each of the three terms.
2. Think about three examples of writing-oriented societies and at least one example of a society (past or present) based on oral culture. Compare and discuss the general uses of each of the two modes of communication in the contexts identified.
3. Why does written English appear to be more lexically sophisticated and complex than speech?
4. Summarise how speech and writing are different using a maximum of ten bullet points for each mode of communication.
5. How do you think knowing how to write has affected your own way of viewing and understanding the world?

Recommendations for Reading

Brown, Gillian and George Yule (1983), *Teaching the Spoken Language: An Approach Based on the Analysis of Conversational English*, Cambridge: Cambridge University Press, pp. 10–16.

Cook, Vivian (2004), *The English Writing System*, London: Arnold, pp. 32–52.

Finnegan, Ruth (2024), *Communicating: The Multiple Modes of Human Communication*, 3rd edn, London and New York: Routledge, pp. 248–251.

Halliday, Michael A. K. (1989), *Spoken and Written Language*, 2nd edn, Oxford: Oxford University Press, pp. 39–45, 61–75, 87.

Meletis, Dimitrios and Christa Dürscheid (2022), *Writing Systems and their Use: An Overview of Grapholinguistics*, Berlin and Boston: De Gruyter Mouton, pp. 14–55.

2 Introducing writing systems

2.1 Typology of writing systems

The previous chapter gave an overview of speech and writing as two different, yet complementary modes of communication. The discussion showed how focusing on one of the two modes of communication inevitably entails studying specific aspects of language and communication. This chapter moves a step further in providing contextual information about the English writing system by introducing writing system typology. In particular, essential definitions are given here in order to identify different categories of writing systems, and to provide a rationale for how scholars have gone about classifying writing systems on the basis of shared and distinct characteristics. The ultimate goal of this discussion is to guide students towards an understanding of where the English writing system is situated within the existing typology of the world's writing systems. In doing so, this chapter also provides a brief summary of the most important work conducted over the past five decades on the structure and function of written English.

According to Coulmas (1996a: 560), a *writing system* is "[a] set of visible or tactile signs used to represent units of language in a systematic way, with the purpose of recording messages which can be retrieved by everyone who knows the language in question and the rules by virtue of which its units are encoded in the writing system […]". In its everyday use, Coulmas continues, the term 'writing system' follows two different strands of meaning. The first type of meaning is that of "the basic types of graphic systems designed to represent language […]". Coulmas explains (1996a: 560) that the other sense is:

> […] what is also referred to as spelling, i.e. a system of rules underlying [written language]. For instance, the English writing system is described as highly involved because its rules operate on different levels of grammatical structure. It is understood in this usage, [Coulmas continues]

> that English writing is alphabetic, but what is meant by 'system' here has to do with how alphabetic letters are combined to represent the phonemes, morphemes and words of English. In this sense a writing system is language specific, being a subsystem of the grammar of a language.

Although it is useful, for the sake of comprehensiveness, to acknowledge the two possible meanings of 'writing system', the use of the term in this textbook corresponds to the first definition provided above – that of a set of signs designed to represent language. The second definition – that of a system of orthographic rules – is assigned, following general practice in writing system research, to the term 'orthography' (see also this textbook's Foreword and Chapter 4, section 4.1). As part of this first definition of a writing system, Coulmas (1996a: 560) makes a distinction between *plerimic* and *cenemic* writing systems, the first containing signs which indicate both sound and meaning, for example the Chinese writing system, and the latter consisting in signs which only indicate sounds but not meaning, for instance the scripts of India.

Classifications like those proposed by Coulmas align with practices from a widely established branch in linguistics, known as 'writing system typology'. In writing system research, *typology* involves theoretically organising writing systems according to their structural features, in order to identify traits which allow one to place individual writing systems within or across different categories (Coulmas, 1996b: 1380; Meletis and Dürscheid, 2022: 211–217). The earliest typological attempts at studying writing systems may be traced back, according to Sproat (2016: 28), to the eighteenth century, when Antoine Court de Gébelin (1775: 399) rudimentarily identified three groups of writing systems among those known at the time: these were 'Chinese', 'Egyptian hieroglyph' and 'alphabetic'. In 1883, Taylor proposed a five-step evolutionary framework that included 'pictures', 'pictorial symbols', 'verbal signs', 'syllabic signs' and 'alphabetic signs' (Joyce and Borgwaldt, 2013: 2).

More in-depth attempts at classifying writing systems were made in the second half of the twentieth century, with the pioneering work of Gelb (1963). He proposed a classification based on the idea that writing systems evolved over time from simple to complex structures, identifying four categories: 'pictographic', 'word syllabic systems', 'syllabaries', and 'segmental alphabets'. Within this framework, pictorial signage and mnemonic devices were considered ancestors of full writing systems (Joyce and Borgwaldt, 2013: 2; Sproat, 2016: 28). Although it encompassed quite a diverse variety of categories, Gelb's writing system classification had some flaws, as it did not allow him to categorise consonant-only writing systems, such as that of Phoenician, as anything other than syllabaries (Sproat, 2016: 28). Those who followed after Gelb in the goal of establishing a typology of writing systems rejected the evolutionary approach to understanding writing systems advanced by him, opting instead for a classification that saw all writing systems in the world as equal in terms of purpose (Joyce and Borgwaldt, 2013: 2; Sproat, 2016: 29).

Sampson (1985) and DeFrancis (1989) in particular established a new hierarchy on the basis of a simple, yet effective, definition of how writing systems operate. In Sampson's view, writing systems are distinguished according to whether they are based solely on meaning ('semasiographic' writing systems) and whether they establish a more explicit connection with phonemes, syllables and morphemes ('glottographic' writing systems). Glottographic writing systems are, in turn, divided into two subcategories, 'logographic' and 'phonographic', where logographs and phonographs are the respective principal units (Sproat, 2016: 29). A *logograph* is a written symbol that has a strong linguistic connection to a word or a morpheme (Coulmas, 1996a: 309). A morpheme is in turn defined as the smallest meaningful linguistic unit (e.g. the word *writes* has two morphemes, *write* + *s*, see Rogers, 2005: 295; Gnanadesikan, 2023: 32; see also Table 2.2 below).[1] A *phonograph*, instead, is a unit in a given writing system that represents a sound or a combination of sounds in a given language (Rogers, 2005: 296; see also Table 2.1 below). Individual sounds, which in linguistics are called 'phonemes', are the smallest distinctive units of sound in a language and allow one to tell apart one word from another (e.g. /p/, /b/, /d/ and /t/ are phonemes in English, as they distinguish words like *pad*, *pat*, *bad* and *bat*) (Rogers, 2005: 296). Phonographs are usually abstract marks indicating one or more phonemes and, as argued by Gnanadesikan (2023: 33), may either be 'pictorial', such as those of Egyptian hieroglyphs, or 'linear', made up of conventional signs, as is the case for most alphabetic writing systems (including English).

Sampson's framework was later challenged by DeFrancis (1989), who claimed that writing systems exclusively based on meaning (semasiographic) may be just a theoretical construct which finds no correspondence in the real world. Sproat (2016: 29) suggests that Blissymbolics[2] may be considered to be an attempt to create a semasiographic

[1] The close correlation between written signs and words or morphemes entails, by definition, the fact that logographs also have a direct correspondence with the semantic aspects of a morpheme or a word (Gnanadesikan, 2023: 32).

[2] A system devised in the twentieth century by Charles K. Bliss for international communication.

writing system. This writing system, however, based on a large number of symbols which indicate a range of relatively simple concepts and which can be combined together with the purpose of indicating other, more complex concepts, has its flaws. As Sproat suggests (2016: 29), Blissymbolics does not express subtle concepts like other writing systems do, and today it is only used as a support communication system for children with learning disabilities. DeFrancis (1989) also disagreed with Sampson's decision to split glottographic writing systems into logographic and phonographic, arguing instead that all writing systems are phonological in nature (Sproat, 2016: 29). In DeFrancis' framework (1989), 'phonological' writing systems are, in turn, divided into 'syllabic' and 'segmental' writing systems, while segmental writing systems branch out into 'consonantal' and 'alphabetic' writing systems.

DeFrancis' typology accounts for a difference between 'pure' writing systems and writing systems that also convey morphological details (Sproat, 2016: 29). An example of the latter type is the Chinese writing system, where both phonological and morphological information is provided concurrently in many of its character units. More recently, DeFrancis' typological framework was criticised by Sproat (2000, later rediscussed in Rogers, 2005, see end of section 2.1), who proposed a planar approach to understanding writing systems in the world, as opposed to the hierarchical structures advanced by Sampson and DeFrancis.

The framework devised by Sproat classifies writing systems according to their type of phonography ('consonantal', 'polyconsonantal', 'alphabetic', 'core syllabic' and 'syllabic'), and accounts for a nuanced gradation of the amount of logography present in each of these types of writing systems. The consonantal, polyconsonantal and alphabetic groups include a graded range of writing systems, from categories where the units contained therein only represent consonants to systems where all (or almost all) elements of a language are represented (Sproat, 2016: 30–31). The core syllabic category indicates writing systems "where the basic symbols generally do represent basic syllables (often just V or CV), but where for more complex syllables one must use a combination of symbols" (Sproat, 2016: 30). The syllabic category, instead, indicates writing systems "where every syllable of the language has one or more separate symbols to represent it" (Sproat, 2016: 30).

The extent to which writing systems are classified as being more or less logographic is, using Sproat's words again (2016: 31), "very impressionistic", in the sense that there is not an objective way of classifying the extent of logography, except for the most obvious cases. While the Chinese writing system is mainly logographic, for example, Japanese has a strong phonographic element to it, but it is still understood as primarily logographic. In the Italian writing system, however, like most other alphabetic writing systems, logography is present only to a small extent (e.g. @ in email addresses or € for the Euro currency). The reason why the logographic dimension is deemed impressionistic is that "some systems whose basic symbols are purely phonetic nonetheless can behave logographically", for example in Perso-Aramaic writing systems (Sproat, 2016: 31). Sproat's theoretical framework can be contextualised on the basis of a few other typological contributions, which came both immediately before and after his own classification, and is witness to a growing interest in identifying similarities and differences across the world's writing systems.

Among the most relevant contributions, there are those by Daniels (2001) and Rogers (2005). Daniels (2001), who may have inspired Sproat's typology, proposed the identification of 'abjads' and 'abugidas' as separate categories, and argued for the identification of six types of writing systems. These are, as reported in Joyce and Borgwaldt (2013: 4),

> (1) logosyllabary (morphosyllabary), (2) syllabary, (3) abjad (Semitic-type script), where each character stands for a consonant, (4) alphabet (Greek-type script), (5) abugida (Sanskrit-type script), where each character stands for a consonant accompanied by a particular vowel, with other vowels indicated by additions to the consonant symbol, and (6) featural, where the shapes of the characters correlate with phonetic features of designated segments.

Rogers (2005), instead, engaged more explicitly with Sproat's work, arguing that the types of phonography identified by Sproat need revising, and proposed a differentiation between 'abjad', 'alphabetic', 'abugida', 'moraic' and 'syllabic' writing systems (Joyce and Borgwaldt, 2013: 5). The category of *moraic* writing systems, which derives its name from the 'mora', an incomplete syllable, is particularly interesting. Rogers (2005: 14) identifies this category as one where the graphic unit indicates a phonological unit in-between a phoneme and a syllable (examples mentioned by Rogers are Cherokee and Cree-Inuktitut). Rogers also replaced the term 'logography' with 'morphography', in order to place the focus not on the word but rather on the morpheme as a principal component of a writing system (Joyce and Borgwaldt, 2013: 5). However, the two terms are still widely used as synonyms (see Meletis and Dürscheid, 2022: 243–244). In 2017, Daniels further updated his typological framework, providing a classification based on 'alphabets', 'abjads' and 'abugidas', which has been defined by Meletis and Dürscheid (2022: 222) as "most influential". Concurrently, however,

Gnanadesikan (2017) criticised Daniels' typology (2001, 2017) suggesting that "abjad-abugida-alphabet-featural script[s] [...] do not acknowledge the similarities between the various scripts that encode segments" (Gnanadesikan, 2017: 19; see also Meletis and Dürscheid, 2022: 223).

In order to address this issue, Gnanadesikan proposed a typology where "alphabets are fully vowelled, abjads are either consonantal or – and this is crucial – partially vowelled, and abugidas are either mostly or fully vowelled. This already highlights that 'abjad' and 'abugida' as defined by Daniels are underdifferentiated types with respect to how the systems assigned to them deal with vowels" (Meletis and Dürscheid, 2022: 223–224). While definitions and classifications are an ongoing topic of discussion and are likely to continue being updated, it is worth taking stock on the basis of existing contributions, the most up-to-date of which is perhaps that from Gnanadesikan (2023). Table 2.1 provides a summary of key definitions based on Gnanadesikan (2023), with examples mostly referring to historical writing systems due to the historical orientation of her chapter.

Table 2.1 Phonographic writing systems (after Gnanadesikan, 2023)

Phonograph A phonograph is "a sign that corresponds to an element (or occasionally more than one element) in the phonology of the language. A phonogram has no inherent semantic meaning" (Gnanadesikan, 2023: 33).
Phonographic writing systems According to Gnanadesikan (2023: 33), at least three groups of phonographs can be identified: *Syllabaries* are writing systems made of syllabograms, phonographic units where there is an obvious correspondence with a syllable – either individual vowels or consonant-vowel combinations (Gnanadesikan, 2023: 33). An example of a syllabary is the Linear B script, the earliest specimen of a writing system in ancient Greek, from about 1400 BC (Gnanadesikan, 2023: 33). *Alphabets* are writing systems where a direct connection with the phoneme (consonant or vowel) exists in its individual graphic components. Phonographic units where there is a direct correlation with an individual phoneme are called letters, as is the case for the *letters* of the Latin alphabet in English (Gnanadesikan, 2023: 33, 41). *Akshara* are a class of writing systems containing a syllable-like unit most frequently used in Brahmic scripts. In Gnanadesikan's words (2023: 33), "[a] simple akshara stands either for a vowel that is not preceded by a consonant (V) or for a consonant followed by a default (unwritten) vowel, which is /a/ in most but not all of the relevant languages. Examples from the Devanāgarī script (used for Hindi, Marathi and Nepali) are उ u and त ta".

Phonographic writing systems, where there is usually a direct relationship between a graphic unit in a given writing system and an individual sound (Rogers, 2005: 296), may also include graphic units representing sounds that do not necessarily always establish an exclusive one-to-one relationship between sounds and letters, but rather make use of a phonetic complement, "a sign that is used in addition to another sign to disambiguate or to re-enforce the pronunciation of that sign" (Gnanadesikan, 2023: 34). Phonemic complements do not have their own sound, but they are entirely dependent on the context in which they are situated; for example, accents may guide the reader to a specific pronunciation of a vowel or, less frequently, a consonant (see Chapter 4, section 4.3). In addition, a writing system may also feature semantic determinatives, which have the sole purpose of specifying "the semantic category of the referent of the sign(s)" with the idea of clarifying its meaning (Gnanadesikan, 2023: 34). This level of connection to meaning is different from that of full logographic systems, which instead operate as summarised in Table 2.2. Again, this table summarises Gnanadesikan's approach (2023) to understanding logographic writing systems.

The parameters given in Tables 2.1 and 2.2 strike a balance between too broad and too narrow a description of writing system features, so that individual categories are distinguished unequivocally, while also

Table 2.2 Logographic writing systems (after Gnanadesikan, 2023)

Logograph A logograph is defined by Gnanadesikan (2023: 32) as "a sign that stands for a word or morpheme of a language" and is "associated with both a meaning and a pronunciation".
Logographic writing systems Typically, a logographic writing system should have a one-to-one relationship between individual signs and individual morphemes, even if these stand for the same lexeme (i.e. a lexical unit behind a group of words which are interconnected via inflection). Thus, for example, *hop*, *hops*, *hopped* and *hopping* would each be represented by a different logograph (compare Gnanadesikan, 2023: 32). In most writing systems, however, one logograph normally represents the core (or the most frequent) morpheme, in this case *hop*, and that is then integrated with the use of phonographs to represent other correlated morphemes (Gnanadesikan, 2023: 32). Logographic systems are not split into subcategories, perhaps due to the relatively small number of examples existing in the world today (Chinese and Japanese kanji). Examples of historical logographic systems include Mesopotamian cuneiform, Egyptian hieroglyphs, the Chinese writing system and Mayan hieroglyphs (Gnanadesikan, 2023: 39–40).

allowing for writing systems to be grouped together. At the same time, however, today's typological classification of writing systems ignores a large number of parameters that could become objects of discussion in future typological frameworks. The examples given by Coulmas (1996b: 1380, as referenced in Meletis and Dürscheid, 2022: 213) still remain valid today, and include structural features such as "chapters, sections, paragraphs, and sentences by means of which text is segmentable", and other, more general qualities like "direction (left, right), axis (horizontal, perpendicular) or lining (top to bottom, bottom to top)".

Other properties include, according to Gnanadesikan (2017: 14–15, as referenced in Meletis and Dürscheid, 2022: 213), the ways in which blank space is used to give meaning to orthography. Including some of these additional parameters in our overall understanding of writing system typologies would have a tangible effect on typological classifications, given the differences existing across the world in the uses of the features above. For example, according to Meletis and Dürscheid (2022: 215), including blank spaces between words as a way to discriminate among individual writing systems would allow placing Chinese, Japanese and Thai in the same unspaced category, in contrast to the rest of the world's writing systems where words are isolated by blank spaces. Such a category of writing systems would not exist without using blank spaces as a key distinguishing criterion.

2.2 Locating written English

The existence of different categories of writing systems in the world is owed to a complex range of linguistic, historical, cultural and pragmatic factors, responding to the needs and uses of individual societies. According to Boyes et al. (2021: 2), a writing system is an expression of social activities ongoing in a given civilisation, in the same way that pottery, culinary practices, religious ceremonies, sports, various forms of art and many other practices are an expression of cultural human activity. Illustrating how writing systems, including that of English, arise from all these variables is a complex task, and one that goes beyond the remits of the present book, since it involves having to take into account contrasting forces and concurring events. However, helpful perspectives for the history of the world's writing systems may be gained from a range of different scholarly publications. The Arabic script, for example, is discussed in Papaconstantinou (2012); the Brahmic scripts in India are examined in Court (1996); cuneiform writing is explored in Glassner (2003); and the Glagolitic writing system (later developed into Cyrillic) is treated in Cubberley (1996).

For the English writing system, matters are no less complex, though some readers may be aware of a general chronology of socio-historical events that might have been taught to them at school. A chronology that follows these general lines might be helpful here, as a way of focusing more closely on the English writing system from this part of the textbook onwards. The most obvious starting point is that of the first settlements of the Anglo-Saxon tribes from about the fifth century AD (Leith, 1997: 13). These early tribes distinguished themselves for their use of runes in inscriptions, as a system to indicate sounds and, therefore, to convey meaning (see the example given in Chapter 1, section 1.2). Another important milestone is that of the spread of Christianity to Ireland first and England later, from about the sixth century AD, which occurred through combined missionary efforts and political strategic choices (Leith, 1997: 16). A third milestone is that of the introduction of the printing press technology in Europe, from the late fifteenth century, which encouraged solutions to make writing more efficient, both for readers and for printers. The need for systematisation, for example, almost immediately caused the disappearance of the thorn (<þ>), and its replacement with <y> or <th> as alternatives to represent /θ/ or /ð/ (Werner, 2019: 81). A fourth milestone is that of the influence of colonisation and globalisation, which is ongoing to the present day, causing the English writing system to move along a pathway of continuous change, in ways that are rather complex.

An immediate example to illustrate this last point is that of the relationship between British English and American English spelling conventions, which, as discussed by Baker (2007), are historically motivated. There is, in particular, a difference in how the American and British cultures have respectively been susceptive to linguistically defining influences. Their different historical trajectories are likely, in principle, still to have an impact on future policies involving the two varieties. Noah Webster had a greater influence on the shaping of American English spelling than any other individual in British English (see Logan, 1937). Over the centuries, American English has also undergone more sustained contact with Mexican Spanish vocabulary than British English, with the consequence that American English word-formation, and, to some degree, spelling, has a more marked inclination towards Mexican Spanish than British English, to accommodate cultural contact (for example, see González, 1995). These examples of linguistic and organisational differences might suggest that American English and British English are likely to continue being subjected to differing pressures in the future, thus increasing their likelihood of becoming more distant from each other than they already are (consider for example, differences in pairs such as *honor/honour* and *authorize/authorise*). With that in mind, one could even pose the question of whether American English spelling will eventually become completely unintelligible from that of British English.[3]

Beyond the specific example of American and British spelling conventions, the peculiar socio-cultural and historical developments of English are responsible for shaping key general features of the English writing system. Beginning with the simplest elements, sentences are written from left to right (with rare exceptions made usually on the internet or advertisement boards for marketing purposes), following a convention established in Latin from around the first century BC. Furthermore, the English writing system uses blank spaces at the edges of each word in order to help readers identify individual words and to facilitate reading, following a convention which was introduced systematically from about the twelfth century AD. Likewise, capital letters are used as a way to indicate the beginning of a new sentence or even to mark differences in meaning (for example *Titanic*, as a proper noun, versus *titanic*, as an adjective; see also Chapter 6, section 6.1), following rules established between the fifteenth and the eighteenth centuries AD. From around the same period, the English writing system also developed a more systematic use of punctuation, in order to complement some of the functions covered by grammar, that is to say, in order to signal sentence structures and to facilitate text processing (compare Cook, 2004: 14–15; see Chapter 5 and Chapter 6).

Although letter-to-sound correspondences were complicated, during the course of history, by developments related to the Great Vowel Shift (see Chapter 1, section 1.3), the English writing system still largely works on the basis that individual graphic units (or a group of them) correspond to one or more phonemes (e.g. the sound /p/ in *pat* or *pile*; more detailed examples are given in Chapter 3). Thus, that of English is an *alphabetic*, and therefore *phonographic*, writing system. Like many other alphabetic systems, however, English uses a mixture of *phonographic and logographic* ways of conveying information (further explanations for these otherwise superficial classifications are made in Chapter 3). The influence of logography in English is evident, for example, in the fact that, during the process of standardisation, English gradually began to

[3] However, these speculations are currently challenged by linguistic evidence (e.g. Baker, 2007), which indicates that the two varieties of written English are actually becoming similar to each another, defining a moment in history – the present – that looks like the peak of a time of saturation in the degree of similarities between American and British English spelling conventions (Baker, 2007: 236).

disambiguate morphologically distinct words using different spelling forms, even if they were essentially homophones. Examples include *bolder* vs. *boulder*, *hole* vs. *whole*, *role* vs. *roll*, *steal* vs. *steel*, *tail* vs. *tale*, *wear* vs. *were* vs. *where*, *waist* vs. *waste* (Sproat, 2016: 36; Ryan, 2016: 45; other examples are provided in Chapter 3, section 3.1).

The primarily phonographic nature of the English writing system is probably the reason why some of the earliest studies aimed at investigating the structure and function of written English were heavily based on the relation between the written and the spoken forms. One of the first contributions to establish a close correlation between the English writing system and phonology is that from Chomsky and Halle (1968). In their book, *The Sound Pattern of English*, the authors provided "many scattered observations" (in the words of Ryan, 2016: 44) about the nature of English in its written form. While mainly focusing on phonology, Chomsky and Halle (1968), later echoed by Noam Chomsky (1970) and Carol Chomsky (1970), also made references to issues inherent to pedagogy, and writing and reading acquisition. As stated by Ryan (2016: 44), all the contributions made up to this point mostly reflected on widespread spelling forms and highly recurring vocabulary; words which are relatively more specialised in meaning and usage received, overall, only sporadic attention.

Venezky's work (1970) was the first to address some of the shortfalls existing in the earliest contributions mentioned above. In particular, Venezky marked a neat separation from other studies (e.g. Hanna et al., 1966; Wijk, 1966; and Albrow, 1972; see Ryan, 2016: 45), where English spelling was studied with the aim of understanding which literacy acquisition methods were more efficient for learning – the 'phonic' method, based on pronunciation, or the 'look-and-say' method, which consisted in remembering the spelling form of a word (Carney, 1994: 86). The American linguist began his work in 1963, with some research on the formation of monomorphemic vocabulary, leading the way to reflecting on the relevance of the morpheme in creating the fabric of written English (Ryan, 2016: 43). Although Venezky began his research activity before Chomsky and Halle, his most acclaimed work is *The Structure of English Orthography*, which was published in 1970. In this book, Venezky focused on a relatively representative set of English words, while also qualitatively drawing on some less frequent spelling patterns (Ryan, 2016: 44).

Venezky's work was informed by structuralist linguistic theories, especially those by Bloomfield (1933) and Hockett (1958). Following their examples, Venezky used the morpheme and the phoneme as points of reference in order to understand spelling patterns, establishing a model for future work focused on the English writing system (Ryan,

2016: 43). Venezky's approach mainly followed a reader-oriented approach, which entailed tracing down all of the steps which led an imaginative reader to establishing a correlation between an individual word form and its correspondent pronunciation, i.e. the spoken form. This approach is in opposition to the writer's perspective, where the person departs from pronunciation first and then translates the phonological understanding of a word into written form (Ryan, 2016: 43). Using the same reader-oriented perspective established in Venezky's first work, *The American Way of Spelling* (Venezky, 1999) further solidified Venezky's authority on English spelling, which remained undisputed for over two decades, when an update on the topic was offered by Carney's *A Survey of English Spelling* (1994).

Carney's book is the first of a series of scholarly publications that are still very much relevant today, as it uses empirical methods which are still considered systematic, easily replicable and reliable. Carney took a more comprehensive reader- and writer-oriented perspective on the English writing system, handling an extensive vocabulary (about 25 million words in total). In his work, Carney took a bold step forward from Venezky, focusing both on the relationship between letters and sounds, in this order, and sound and spelling, in this sequence. By taking both angles, the book attempted to overview some of the efforts made both in the act of constructing and also in the act of comprehending English spelling (Ryan, 2016: 44).

While providing a detailed assessment of the work accomplished by Venezky (1970) and Chomsky and Halle (1968), Carney conducted, in his attempt to map speech-to-text and text-to-speech correlations, a frequency-based study of all examples of both types of correlation, and their relationship with word frequencies. Ryan (2016: 44) mentions one of the most interesting findings of this type of analysis, namely the fact that there are relatively few words where the spelling <gh> equals the sound /f/, but those words that feature it are core, highly-recurring lexical units in English vocabulary (e.g. the word *rough*). Conversely, <ff> corresponds to /f/ in many more lexical items of lower frequency (e.g. *Buffalos*).

Another relevant attempt at understanding the nature of the English writing system is that made by Rollings, whose thoughts are summarised in *The Spelling Patterns of English* (2004). In the book, the author established regularities in the spelling of English and discovered that, although it is characterised by apparent chaos and complexity, some systematic patterns can be found if we compare spellings with sounds. In particular, Rollings made a case for the value of using syllable division for indicating vowels and how vowels can be understood according to different orthographic criteria (Ryan, 2016: 44). The book also contains references to examples of orthographic regularities – frequently recurring spelling patterns – present in English vocabulary, similar to those to be described in Chapter 3, section 3.2 in this textbook. While a purely phonological perspective on English spelling had long been abandoned by the time Rollings wrote his book, his contribution represents an insightful update on the traditional approach offered by the previous generation of scholars mentioned earlier in this section.

One of the most recent efforts in the study of the English writing system is the work conducted by Ryan (2018). The approach taken in Ryan's doctoral dissertation consists of the analysis of a range of different spelling examples, looking in particular into more complex cases where morphological and phonological information overlap. Examples include position-specific changes in word spellings, for instance word-endings used in order to mark a grammatical feature such as case and tense, known as 'inflection' (e.g. *-ed*, *-ing* and *-s*); the formation of entirely new words conducted by using suffixes, known as 'derivation' (e.g. *electric* > *electricity* > *electrician*); as well as a number of proper names and non-standard spellings (e.g. *Cook*/*Cooke* and *boyz*, respectively).

In Ryan's thesis (2018: 79–87), four different principles of spelling formation are explored, notably the *identity principle*, the *phonographic matching principle*, the *distinctiveness principle* and the *invariance principle* (see Chapter 3, section 3.3), and it is argued that these four principles apply pervasively to all spelling forms available in English. However, in a number of non-traditional examples of complex spelling categories examined in Ryan's thesis, called "peripheral spelling" forms (Ryan, 2018: 61), the proportions of occurrence and interaction of the four principles are different from what they would be for all other English words. While being interesting even just for these suggestions alone, Ryan's thesis also provides valuable insights into how standard spelling inhibits creative efforts and how creative spelling can give us information about the mechanisms underlying standard spelling. Ryan's work concludes with a thought-provoking statement about our understanding of the English writing system within the typological framework discussed in this chapter. In one of his concluding paragraphs, the author (Ryan, 2018: 345–346) affirms that, while

> base forms [in English spelling] may be broadly phonemic, as Venezky (1970) states, we can now see that semantic relations are expressed through the recurrence of letter-strings [e.g. *dearest* < *dear* vs. *deerhunter* < *deer*]. Thus new spellings are generally formed out of existing units of spelling, and this creates a web of interconnections that cannot be

explained by viewing the writing system as a series of correspondences between spelling and sound.

Further thoughts on this statement are offered in Chapter 3.

Discussion Material

1. Find some of the most important similarities and differences existing among all proposals of typology of writing systems discussed in section 2.1 and discuss your findings with your class.
2. How do the theories put forward by Sampson (1985) and DeFrancis (1989) differ, and how do they compare with the proposals made by Sproat (2000) and Rogers (2005)?
3. What are the definitions of phonographic and logographic writing systems, in your own words?
4. Create a diagram in order to summarise how the studies on the English writing system summarised in section 2.2 are related to and build on each other.
5. What do you think are some theoretical areas of investigation that have not yet been explored in the English writing system, which would be a welcome addition to the field?

Recommendations for Reading

Gnanadesikan, Amalia (2023), 'Classifying and comparing early writing systems', in Marco Condorelli and Hanna Rutkowska (eds), *The Cambridge Handbook of Historical Orthography*, Cambridge: Cambridge University Press, pp. 29–49.

Joyce, Terry and Susanne Borgwaldt (2013), 'Typology of writing systems: Introduction', in Terry Joyce and Susanne Borgwaldt (eds), *Typology of Writing Systems*, Amsterdam and Philadelphia: John Benjamins, pp. 1–11.

Meletis, Dimitrios and Christa Dürscheid (2022), *Writing Systems and their Use: An Overview of Grapholinguistics*, Berlin and Boston: De Gruyter Mouton, pp. 210–269.

Ryan, Des (2016), 'Linguists' descriptions of the English writing system', in Vivian Cook and Des Ryan (eds), *The Routledge Handbook of the English Writing System*, London: Routledge, pp. 43–45.

Sproat, Richard (2016), 'English among the writing systems of the world', in Vivian Cook and Des Ryan (eds), *The Routledge Handbook of the English Writing System*, London: Routledge, pp. 27–40.

3 A complex writing system

3.1 Morpheme-based spelling

The previous chapter gave an introduction to writing system typology, describing some of the most important proposals made to date in order to identify similarities and differences across writing systems in the world. In an attempt to place the English writing system within the existing typology of writing systems, Chapter 2 summarised existing scholarship focused on the structure and function of English orthography. This chapter moves a step further in the same direction, providing additional insights, drawn from relevant literature, which contribute to outlining a profile of the English writing system as indeed primarily phonographic, but with a unique degree of complexity. As evidenced by the discussion provided in Chapter 2, spelling arrangements in English are sometimes not simply the result of direct correspondences between sound and spelling – which makes English orthography unusually difficult (Ryan, 2018: 345–346).

According to Sproat (2016: 31), the English writing system is not only "quirky and unpredictable", but, as demonstrated in quantitative research such as that by van den Bosch et al. (1994), may be considered the most complex Western writing system, because of its irregular relationships between letters and sounds. An important factor underlying the existence of complex correlations between spelling forms and pronunciations is the fact that, as Henderson and Chard (1980: 111) suggest, even for just a simple word such as *fake*, readers have to choose, in principle, between about nineteen different ways in which individual sounds can be lined up together, and twenty-seven different ways in which the four letters can be arranged to form the word (Carney, 1994: 16–18). The variety of combinations in which letter-to-sound correspondences can be made in English creates, at least in theory, a scenario where several different sounds may be represented by an individual word spelling. A widely cited example from George Bernard Shaw

(Stubbs, 1980: front cover, as quoted in Neuman, 2023: 634) to illustrate the point is that of *ghoti*, an unusual but logically possible way of spelling 'fish', if we consider the fact that <gh> can indicate, in English, /f/ (e.g. in *enough*), <o> can stand for /ɪ/ (e.g. in *women*) and <ti> can represent /ʃ/ (e.g. in *nation*).

Clearly, *ghoti* gains its intended hilarity from the fact that, as most will know, it is an 'impossible' spelling (Carney, 1994: 21). The case of *ghoti* is an example of our "temptation to overstate irregularities" existing in the English writing system (Carney, 1994: 16). For this reason, context is crucial in resolving ambiguities arising from all the possible mapping options that involve sound-to-letter and letter-to-sound correspondences (Carney, 1994: 17). In particular, word context helps us to understand that individual letter positions have an influence on the likelihood of that letter being pronounced as a particular sound rather than another. As one may guess from the few word examples given above with reference to the spelling of *ghoti*, <gh> for /f/ is only possible word-finally, <o> for /ɪ/ is only available in *women*, and <ti> for /ʃ/ is only found in word-medial positions. Word context also allows us to understand that individual phonemes are not always represented, in written English, "one letter at a time" (Carney, 1994: 17). In the word *fake*, for example, word-final <e> is crucial for allowing us to understand the phonetic value of word-medial <a>, which is /eɪ/ rather than /æ/ or /ʌ/ (further details about spelling arrangements and constraints, known as *graphotactics*, are available in Chapter 4, section 4.3).

So far, we have seen examples that illustrate how letter-to-sound correspondences complicate the ways in which the English writing system works as a phonographic writing system. As briefly mentioned in Chapter 2 (section 2.2), however, complexity in the English writing system also arises from the fact that, while being a primarily phonological writing system, English vocabulary blends phonographic and logographic information in a way that is unique in the world's alphabetic writing systems. While "[t]he alphabetic principle [...] requires [...] that a given phoneme is represented by a constant symbol [and] that the symbol involved does not represent other phonemes" (Carney, 1994: 15), English vocabulary permits, as briefly seen in Chapter 2 (section 2.2) through different examples, the coexistence of forms where different spelling forms for the same sound string carry different meanings, e.g. *to*, *two* and *too* (pronounced as /tuː/). Other examples are *cite*, *sight* and *site* (/saɪt/); *peek*, *peak* and *pique* (/piːk/); and *pair*, *pear* and *pare* (/pɛə/). Road signs are additional examples of words where the intersection between phonography and logography is particularly visible, as a solution driven by the need to provide information quickly and efficiently. An illustrative example would be that of *deer xing* for 'deer crossing', where the *x* stands as a logogram for 'cross' rather than as a phonograph for /ks/.

The amount of logography present in the English writing system encourages further reflection about the extent to which morpheme-based spelling frameworks have driven efforts to understand English orthography. The focus on the morpheme is a watershed topic that frequently characterises new-generation work not only in theoretical discourses about the English writing system, as seen in Chapter 2, but also in strictly focused, well-defined case studies. In 2017, Berg and Aronoff showed that there are regularities in the ways in which derivational suffixes *-ous*, *-ic*, *-al* and *-y* are used in their consistent spelling forms to avoid homophony. In light of these findings, they argued that, as evidenced in previous work (Bolinger, 1946; Chomsky and Halle, 1968; Venezky, 1999: 197ff.), English orthography builds upon lexical and morphological principles that are normally not as heavily present in other alphabetic writing systems (Berg and Aronoff, 2017: 61–62). Shortly after this statement was made, however, Berg and Aronoff published a second article (2021) in which they claimed that, while the English writing system "encodes individual suffixes at the expense of phonological transparency", there appears to be "no evidence for anything more than historical accident" to prove that English "orthography distinguishes homophonous monomorphemic stems systematically" (Berg and Aronoff, 2021: 327).[1] Another passage from the same article (Berg and Aronoff, 2021: 315) illuminates what the two authors mean by 'homophonous monomorphemic stems' and adds details about their approach to understanding the nature of historical English spelling. In particular, it explains that the authors used the CELEX database (Baayen et al., 1995) and also drew on historical printed dictionaries in order to scope out the extent to which English vocabulary showed homophony across word roots (e.g. *bank* vs. *bank* and *pair* vs. *pear* vs. *pare*) (Berg and Aronoff, 2021: 315). The authors then went on to count the number of roots with discrete spelling forms and found out that they amounted to less than half of the overall number of their results (Berg and Aronoff, 2021: 315). These findings show that "[h]istorically, it appears that in many cases we are not dealing with a graphemic differentiation of stems, but with a conservation of spellings" (Berg and Aronoff, 2021: 315).

The lesson learned from Berg and Aronoff is simple but important. Identifying the morpheme as a foundation of spelling patterns in the

[1] For a definition of 'homophonous', see Chapter 4, section 4.3.

English writing system "is far from a complete model of English spelling but it is also far from wrong" (Ryan, 2016: 47). This approach, Ryan continues on the same page, gives us some pointers to the inner mechanisms of the English writing system, showing how orthography establishes correlations between words and their semantic values, in the face of otherwise confusing changes in pronunciation. At the same time, however, the way in which logography operates in an alphabetic system like that of written English is not foolproof. As Sampson (1985: 201) already argued decades ago, pairs like *speak* vs. *speech*, *palace* vs. *palatial*, *joke* vs. *jocular*, *collide* vs. *collision* and *prodigal* vs. *prodigious* (this last pair being etymologically unrelated) are all proof that morphemic consistency fails, due to the variation in spelling existing between items in each pair. Thus, statements such as those made by Chomsky and Halle, who argued that the English writing system is "a near optimal system for the lexical representation of English words" (1968: 49), should be taken with extreme caution.

While research on the interaction between phonography and logography in the English writing system is still ongoing, the insights provided by Berg and Aronoff (2021) alert us to the fact that there are complex interactions between phonographic and morphological elements in English orthography, but the extent to which either prevails heavily depends on the individual morphological segments under analysis. This complicated scenario makes it difficult to describe the English writing system as anything more than 'something in between alphabetic and logographic'. However, a concept first developed in the mid-twentieth century and further refined during the 1970s and the 1980s (e.g. by Kavanagh and Mattingly, 1974; Katz and Feldman, 1983), that of *orthographic depth*, has helped scholars to establish a clearer relationship between the English writing system and other alphabetic writing systems. Orthographic depth is defined by Tamošiūnaitė (2023: 83) as "a scalar dimension that intends to capture the regularity and consistency of mappings between graphic signs and related linguistic levels" (see also Rogers, 2005: 295). The level of complexity in which an alphabetic writing system can convey sound-related information creates a distinction between *deep* and *shallow* orthographies. The two polar values indicate writing systems where accessibility, dictated by the correlation between spellings and their phonological representation, is more or less complex. In particular, shallow orthographies are writing systems where there is a direct one-to-one relationship between sounds and spellings, and are called 'shallow' because the correlation between spelling and pronunciation is more explicit (Rogers, 2005: 177; Tamošiūnaitė, 2023: 83–84).

Deep orthographies, instead, provide a more indirect relationship between sounds and spellings and therefore obscure our understanding of how individual words are pronounced on the basis of their written form (Rogers, 2005: 177; Tamošiūnaitė, 2023: 83–84). As argued by Tamošiūnaitė (2023: 83–84), labelling orthographies 'deep' or 'shallow' is a problematic approach in its definition, as it stems from an outdated assumption that the morphological level of orthographic signalling is more idealised (hence 'deep') while the phonological level is more pragmatic (thus, 'shallow'). Moreover, the notion of orthographic depth was originally devised exclusively for the purposes of investigating reading performances from the perspective of the psychology of reading (Joyce, 2023: 156). While being tricky in its original understanding, however, the deep and shallow dichotomy has been an effective instrument for scholars to measure the considerable influence of the morpheme in an alphabetic writing system like that of English. Within this framework, the English writing system is seen, by those involved in writing system theory, as having a deep level of phonological representation, if placed in comparison with other related languages.

To give some additional, contextualising examples, Italian and Finnish are shallow orthographies, because there is always a consistent correspondence between letters indicating consonants and vowels on one hand, and their respective pronunciations on the other hand. Examples include Italian *luna* for 'moon' (/luːna/) and Finnish *kuu* for 'moon' (/kuː/), where each letter corresponds to an individual sound. In contrast to these examples, French has, much like English, a deep orthography, since the pronunciation of some letters corresponding to consonants and vowels may change depending on context, word history, etymology and semantics. Additionally, some French words have a spelling that appears redundant, in terms of overall sound-to-spelling correlations, when compared to actual word pronunciation: the <e> in *lune*, for example, does not correspond to any sound in its spoken form /lyn/ 'moon'. While both English and French are on the deeper end of the orthographic depth spectrum, and are therefore deemed to be more complex among the world's alphabetic writing systems in terms of sound-to-letter correspondences, scholars have not held back from seeking to establish order in the midst of their complexities in a number of ways. The following sections discuss examples applicable to English.

3.2 Capturing complexity

The extent of complexity existing in the English writing system has been captured by scholars like Cook (2004: 55) in the form of a series of "rules for English spelling that can be stated quite readily, at least as rough approximations". These spelling rules, Cook continues (2004: 55), "illustrate general properties of English that mostly go unnoticed and demonstrate how English spelling depends on particular aspects of English phonology and grammar as well as on correspondence rules".[2] The rules in question are expressed as the 'three-letter rule', the '<th> rule', the 'surname rule' and the 'consonant doubling rule'. They are summarised, on the basis of the descriptions provided by Cook (2004: 56–61), in Table 3.1 below.

Table 3.1 Spelling rules (according to Cook, 2004: 56–61)

Three-letter rule

The three-letter rule consists in marking a distinction between *content* words (words which have a meaning, including nouns, verbs and adjectives) and *function* words (words with a primarily grammatical function, such as prepositions and pronouns) (Cook, 2004: 38). This rule generally helps with distinguishing words of different classes that have the same sound by spelling them differently, for example *by* and *buy* or *aw* and *awe*. In these examples, three-letter words are content words, whereas two-letter words are function words. In all other cases where homophony does not occur, function words may be represented by a spelling form that is longer than two letters, for example in *moreover* and *albeit*. All words with a spelling form of one or two letters only, however, are always function words (Cook, 2004: 56–57).

The <th> rule

Much like the three-letter rule, the <th> rule entails the fact that different rules apply to different word categories in English vocabulary. In function words like *them* and *these*, <th> corresponds to the sound /ð/, while in words like *thunder*, *thirst* and *theory*, which are content words, it represents the sound /θ/. The <th> rule is fairly consistent in English vocabulary, especially in word examples where the <th> spelling is found in word-initial position, such as those provided above. Exceptions to the <th> rule include words where <th> actually corresponds to /t/, e.g. *Thailand*. In word examples where <th> occurs in positions other than word-initially (word-medially and word-finally), one may more frequently find /ð/, for example in *bother* and *mother*, /θ/, like in *moth* and *Matthew*, or /t/, as in the compound words *pothole* and *foothill* (Cook, 2004: 57–58).

[2] While Cook switches between 'properties' and 'rules' to refer to the patterns summarised in Table 3.1, this chapter makes a distinction between *rules* (explained in section 3.2) and *properties* (section 3.3). Spelling rules are understood as fixed guidelines, while spelling properties establish more general patterns of organisational behaviour.

Table 3.1 (continued)

The surname rule

The surname rule consists in visually distinguishing surnames from other words that would otherwise sound and look exactly like a person's surname. This rule is implemented by means of a range of different solutions, for example that of repeating the final letter of a word, while also using capitalisation, in pairs like *cob* vs. *Cobb*, *web* vs. *Webb* and *but* vs. *Butt.* Another solution consists in adding <e> word-finally to the spelling of a capitalised surname, as in the case of *sharp* vs. *Sharpe*, or by mixing the two solutions explained above, like in *don* vs. *Donne* and *man* vs. *Manne.* Another approach involves the replacement of <i> with <y>, concurrently with using a word-final <e> whenever the capitalised word ends with a consonant (compare, for instance, *miles* vs. *Myles* and *wild* vs. *Wylde*) (Cook, 2004: 58).

As argued by Cook (2004: 59), spelling variation in surnames was, in the past, a great deal more frequent than it is today. An example is that of the name of Shakespeare, which appears in several different spelling variants in his historical works, including *Shakes-speare*, *Shakespear*, *Shakespere* and *Shakspere* (examples available in Brown, 2019: 75). The variation was owed to the fact that, in the past, the person who owned the surname felt entitled to spell it however they wanted (Cook, 2004: 59). A comparable case may also be found in place names, for instance *Bicester* and *Leominster*, respectively pronounced /ˈbɪstər/ and /ˈlɛmstər/, though there may be more complex sound changes underlying these examples (Cook, 2004: 59).

Consonant doubling

The consonant doubling rule consists in the repetition of individual consonants in specific linguistic contexts, for example, in conjunction with the use of suffixes such as *-ing*, *-er*, *-ed* and *-est.* Here, consonant doubling occurs in between the base and the suffix, so for example in *beginning*, *potter*, *cupped* and *hottest.* In all examples given above, consonant doubling does not automatically lead to a lengthening in the pronunciation of the consonant letter being duplicated. There is, however, a relationship between consonant doubling and the pronunciation of vowels in the vicinity of the consonants being duplicated. If the consonant following a vowel is double, then the vowel is short; if it is single, and sometimes followed by word-final <e>, the vowel is long (Cook, 2004: 60). Examples include the words *vale* vs. *valley*, *tape* vs. *tapper* and *save* vs. *savvy.* Some consonants are doubled infrequently, for example <v> and <k>, while others are not doubled at all, for instance <w> and <x>. Crucially, consonant doubling does not always consist in the repetition of the same letter; rather, spelling clusters of different letters may work as a doubled version of a single consonant. Examples of this kind include <ck>, e.g. in *tracking* (compare the use of <c> in *trace*) and <dge>, e.g. in *judge* (compare the use of <u> in *jury*) (Cook, 2004: 59–61).

Note: Some of these examples go beyond those available in Cook (2004: 58–59) and are based on the information provided in the author's personal web page, which integrates his textbook (<http://www.viviancook.uk/EnglishSpellingSystem/SurnameRules.htm> [accessed February 2024]).

The contents of Table 3.1 represent only a minority of all of the possible spelling patterns existing in the English writing system, some of which are more difficult to define as rules than others. A compelling example given by Cook (2004: 54), Carney (1994: 15) and further discussed by Crystal (2012: 177–185) is that of the spelling <ie>, which illustrates the complexity of spelling patterns in the English writing system, and our difficulty with describing them by means of boxed-up rules or jingles.

For decades in the past, Crystal notes, children in school were taught a rule that goes more or less as follows: '*i* before *e*, except after *c*, and if you please, the little word *seize*'. Alternatively, the following was used: '*i* before *e*, except after *c*, or when sounded like *a*, as in *neighbour* and *weigh*' (Crystal, 2012: 177). These rules were devised in order to help students to learn correct spelling, while avoiding confusion generated by the many possible sound values behind <ie>. The primary sound indicated by <ie> is /iː/, for example in *grief*, *relieved*, *chief*, *yield* and *achievement*. Other sound values which may also be represented by <ie>, albeit less frequently, are /ɪə/, as in *frontiersman* and *courtier*, or /aɪ/, as in *tie* and *die*. Additional, rarer sound correspondences include /aɪə/, for instance in *signifier*, *dietary* and *societal*; /iːe/, as in *Vienna*; /juː/, as in *view*; and /e/, as in *friend* (Crystal, 2012: 179–180).

While the sound correspondences of <ie> may already be complex, additional issues arise with the <ei> spelling, which is visually and phonologically closely connected with <ie>, as this may also correspond to /iː/ in words such as *deceit* and *conceivable*. Thus, Crystal continues (2012: 180), the rule established above should be reframed as something along the lines of '*i* before *e*, except after *c*, when the spelling represents /iː/'. Even at this point, however, the <ie> rule needs further revision, due to the presence, in English, of suffix-related changes owed to grammatical rules. Some of the required modifications need to take into account the fact that nouns with a word-final <y> normally turn to <ies> (e.g. *grammy* → *grammies*) in the plural form and <ies> and <ied> in the third person present and the past tense respectively (e.g. *pry* → *pries*, *pried*). Comparable developments can also be encountered in suffixed adjectival forms, e.g. *early*, *earlier*, *earliest* (Crystal, 2012: 180).

Perhaps because of the influence of the grammatical forms explained above, the <ie> spelling took up a strong grammatical marking value in English, which operates beyond orthographic constraints. Today, it is not unusual to see some of the developments explained above also among words featuring a preceeding <c>, as in *supremacies*, *emergencies*, *diplomacies* and *tendencies*. Crystal (2012: 181) also mentions a few adjectives and verbs as relevant examples, for instance *racier*, *juiciest* and *fancied* (examples from Crystal, 2012: 181). At this point, the rule would inevitably have to be amended once again to something along the lines of '*i* before *e*, except after *c*, unless the *c* appears before an ending which indicates a change in the form of a noun, a verb or an adjective' (Crystal, 2012: 181). With that said, one should also account for words featuring a <c> in their root morpheme, which generate cognate words with longer spelling forms by attaching different suffixes to it. Examples include forms like *proficient*, where the *profic-* part can be connected to different elements to form *proficiently*, *proficiency*, *proficience*, and so on (examples from Crystal, 2012: 181). English vocabulary has enough words of the type exemplified here to require an adjustment to the rule from which Crystal departed to illustrate the complex case of <ie> in English.

With the new exceptions, the revised rule would be as follows: '*i* before *e*, except after *c*, unless the *c* appears before an ending which builds up a larger word' (Crystal, 2012: 181). But that, once again, is still not enough for a fully exhaustive description of the correct way of spelling <ie> amidst the intricacies of English vocabulary. The counterpart of the <ie> spelling, <ei>, which, as mentioned, also corresponds to /iː/, actually appears to be just as complex as <ie> when it comes to its behaviour following <c>. In French loanwords, in particular, the rule that <ei> only follows <c> is not always respected: examples include words like *forfeit* (/ˈfɔːfɪt/), *seize* (/siːz/), *vein* (/veɪn/), *beige* (/beɪʒ/), *rein* (/reɪn/), *heir* (/ɛː(r)/) and *reign* (/reɪn/) (examples from Crystal, 2012: 182).[3] In addition to words derived from French, there are also other words in English vocabulary that are not connected in any way to French and yet constitute exceptions to the rule established for the <ei> spelling. These include, for example, the words *weird*, *either*, *neither*, *eight* (and its derivatives *eighteen*, *eighty*, and so on), which each have their own individual, peculiar history (examples from Crystal, 2012: 182–184).

The complexity arising from attempting to establish ad-hoc rules, following the example given by Crystal, is at least part of the reason why contemporary scholars tend to favour a focus on *principles*, rather than rules, to explain spelling behaviour in the English writing system. The ultimate goal of principles, intended as broader, more flexible guiding patterns, rather than fixed sets of instructions, is that of establishing a framework that leaves out fewer stranding exceptions. While comprehensiveness may always be undermined by the peculiar history of each word in English vocabulary, Ryan's principles of English spelling, briefly referenced to in Chapter 2 (section 2.2), and fully described in

[3] For words like these, the term 'rule' is perhaps misleading, and it would be preferable to refer to 'memory aids', given the various pronunciations and the *c*-less spelling.

section 3.3 below, provide a helpful head start on the task of understanding regularities in the English writing system.

3.3 Principles of English spelling

The reason why written English seems so difficult to understand systematically is that there is a conflict among different principles regulating the ways in which English orthography works. In an attempt to understand these principles, Ryan (2016: 53–57; 2018: 79–87) proposes a theoretical framework that departs from Cummings (1988) and DeFrancis (1989). According to Cummings (1988: 12–24), English spelling is the result of contrastive 'precepts', consisting in acoustic, semantic and visual regulatory forces. Thus, to give an example, the sound precept requires that <g> is normally spelled and pronounced /g/ or /ʤ/ (e.g. in *gigantic*) while the semantic precept requires that semantically related words like *sign*, *signed* and *signature* have a consistent <g> spelling even though <g> does not always correspond to a /g/ or a /ʤ/ sound (other examples available in Ryan, 2018: 80). In Cummings' theory (1988: 21–24), the visual precept is another force responsible for shaping English spelling; it establishes the fact that spelling requires a degree of predictability and coherence detectable by the eye (Ryan, 2018: 80; compare section 3.1).

The visual precept, Cummings argues, has gradually prevailed over the acoustic one, where words must be coherent in their letter-to-sound correlations. According to Cummings, the shift mentioned above occurred as a result of the introduction of the printing press in England during the late fifteenth century, when a growing number of people developed a taste for reading quietly in their own time (Ryan, 2018: 80; see Chapter 5, section 5.2). The advantage of silent reading was that visual regularity could be understood by everyone, regardless of their geographical location and the regional variety of English that they spoke. A category of English spelling in which the prevalence of the visual over the acoustic precept is particularly obvious is that of etymological spelling (see also this textbook's Foreword). The word *signature*, which has just been mentioned above with reference to the semantic force, is also a relevant example of etymological spelling, where the <g> spelling, a Late Middle English addition based on Latin *signum* [ˈsɪŋnʊ̃], led to pronouncing the word with a /g/ (example adapted from Ryan, 2016: 54; 2018: 80).

According to DeFrancis (1989) – who, as we have seen in Chapter 2, section 2.1, argued that all writing systems are primarily phonological – English orthography is also regulated by tradition. In other words,

DeFrancis emphasises the importance of spelling habits inherited from the past, and how these have contributed to creating a gap between the written form and pronunciation (Ryan, 2018: 79–80).

Building upon Cummings and DeFrancis, Ryan (2016: 53–56; 2018: 81–87) proposes four principles of English orthography, namely the *identity principle*, the *phonographic matching principle*, the *distinctiveness principle*, and the *invariance principle*. The most important of these is the *identity principle*, which, echoing the claim made by Cummings about the 'visual' nature of spelling, indicates the fact that word spellings tend towards establishing visual regularity with other existing, related words in English vocabulary (Ryan, 2016: 53–54; 2018: 83). The reason why Ryan does not call this principle 'visual' is that it applies not only to sight-based writing systems like that of English but also to touch-based ones such as Morse code and audio-related ones like those accompanying traffic lights (Ryan, 2016: 54).

The identity principle is considered by Ryan as most important because it can be applied to a larger number of words in English vocabulary than the other categories. Abbreviations follow the identity principle, especially when the short forms are visual, not necessarily phonetically accurate renditions of their respective longer word spellings. Relevant examples include abbreviations for days of the week, e.g. *Mon*, *Tue*, *Wed*, which stand for *Monday*, *Tuesday*, *Wednesday*, and do not necessarily abbreviate the ways in which these words are pronounced, namely /mʌndeɪ/, /ˈtjuːzdeɪ/ (British English pronunciation) and /ˈwɛnzdeɪ/ (examples from Ryan, 2016: 54). The examples above are, to be more precise, instances of 'clipping', a type of abbreviation which occurs when a full word form is truncated, removing one or more syllables from the original spelling form. Another clipping example affected by the identity principle is that of *veg* for 'vegetables' (example from Carney, 1994: 105, as cited in Ryan, 2018: 328).

In addition to clippings, Ryan argues (2018: 83), inflections and etymological spellings are also affected by the identity principle. A set of inflections that follow the identity principle would be those related to the verb *to jump*, such as the forms <jump+s>, <jump+ing> and <jump+ed>, the last example clearly following visual similarity despite its different pronunciation in the past tense, /jʌmpt/ (examples from Ryan, 2018: 90). Examples of etymological words abiding to the identity principle are those with easily identifiable morphemic or lexical subunits, such as *misdoubt* and *doubted*, both of which have a clear connection with *doubt* (see also this textbook's Foreword; other examples available in Ryan, 2016: 53–54; 2018: 83). The way in which etymological spellings are affected by the identity principle is somewhat more complex, as explained in the following quote from Ryan (2018: 334):

> Adoptions without adaptation, such as *gateau* and *macchiato*, occur when the identity of the borrowed word's spelling is preserved whole; and adoptions with adaptation, such as *philosophy*, *larval* and *possible*, where a word has been borrowed from another language (often a combination of French and Latin) but its spelling has been adapted somewhat to fit in with [the] English writing system.

The second principle discussed by Ryan (2016: 54–55; 2018: 83–84) is the *phonographic matching principle*. This principle states that word spellings are regulated on the basis of a connection between the written form and its pronunciation, a process which is indeed called 'phonographic matching' (Ryan, 2016: 54; 2018: 83). The principle may apply, for example, to proper names, when these are borrowed from a foreign language which makes spelling, and its correlated pronunciation, obscure (compare the revised form *The Pogues* – the name of a late twentieth-century Celtic punk band – from Gaelic *Póg mo Thóin* 'kiss my arse' to indicate /pəʊg/; the spelling may well have been inspired by the spelling of the English word *vogue* (example adapted from Ryan, 2016: 54–55; 2018: 83–84). This second principle is not in contrast with the identity principle, but it accommodates visual cues in order to ensure that the visual form of a word also conveys helpful sound-related information. Thus, spelling arrangements in English orthography are the product of a delicate balance between the identity principle and the phonographic matching principle.

However, while in theory the phonographic matching principle should always agree with the identity principle, Ryan argues, this is frequently not the case, with the exception of rare spelling categories such as those of words formed directly from pronunciation (e.g. *kangaroo*; Ryan, 2016: 54–55; 2018: 83–84). Morphemic consistency sometimes overrides phonetic regularity, so as to allow for spellings such as *sane* and *sanity*, *mine* and *mimic*, *cone* and *conical*, *diabetes* and *diabetic*, *divine* and *divinity*, *profane* and *profanity*, *know* and *knowledge*, to have relatively consistent and predictable spellings (examples from Carney, 1994: 18; Coulmas, 1996a: 348; compare the examples given in section 3.1). A similar pattern occurs in inflections such as *-ed*, which are graphically consistent in English but indicate slightly different pronunciations depending on the root to which they are attached, such as in *wanted* /ˈwɒntɪd/ and *wished* /wɪʃt/ (Coulmas, 1996a: 348; other examples available in Ryan, 2016: 54; 2018: 83–84).

The third principle discussed by Ryan is the *distinctiveness principle*, which indicates that individual words should be identifiable by their own unique spelling forms (Ryan, 2016: 55; 2018: 82). While this rule applies automatically to words phonetically and semantically distant from each other, for example *sun* and *moon*, it is especially important for words where pronunciation and spelling forms are close enough to potentially cause ambiguity. For instance, word spellings of pairs such as *here* and *hear*, or *desert* and *dessert*, are respectively similar in spelling but different semantically (compare Chapter 2, section 2.2). Additional examples are *in* vs. *inn* (preposition vs. noun) and *be* vs. *bee* (verb vs. noun), where different spellings signal different word classes (see section 3.1 on the distinction between content and function words) (Ryan, 2016: 55–56; 2018: 82). Although all the examples covered so far stem from practical needs to disambiguate words, there are also examples of words where the distinctiveness principle applies for reasons other than purely linguistic. In particular, names such as *Kleen Brite* and *Gorillaz* (examples from Ryan, 2016: 55) appear to be the result of conscious marketing choices, aimed at striking a peculiar, original impression in the public mind.

While the distinctiveness principle applies far and wide, English is rife with ambiguous cases where individual word spellings have two or more meanings. Examples include *lead* ('to guide' or 'a metal'), *produce* ('to make' or 'fruit and vegetables') and *sewer* ('drainage system' or 'one who sews'), for which context is usually the only way to identify the exact meaning. Other examples include the forms *sin* ('a moral error', 'abbreviation for Latin *sine*', 'Arabic letter') and *mobile* ('a phone', 'able to move freely and easily', 'decorative structure suspended in the air') (definitions as available on *Oxford Languages*). The reasons why examples like those given above do not follow the distinctiveness principle are most varied: sometimes, homographs develop from an individual word that strands out into different meanings; other times, different historical word roots merge into the same spelling form, either casually or by analogy (see also Ryan, 2016: 55–56).

The last of the four principles discussed by Ryan is the *invariance principle*, which states that spellings have a tendency to crystallise in form (Ryan, 2016: 56; 2018: 86–87). To illustrate the point, Ryan (2016: 56) gives the examples of *was* and *wag*, both of which retain the spelling <a> even though they each have a different vowel, /wɒz/ vs. /wæg/. As a result of the invariance principle, the spellings of some words, already affected by the distinctiveness principle, are reinforced as distinct even if they have the same sound, for example *pray* vs. *prey* and *feet* vs. *feat.* To complement the point made at the end of the previous paragraph, the visual distinction of words that are otherwise pronounced the same is owed to a long and complex process of development in the history of English, involving overlapping forces like those of the mechanics of the printing press and the Great Vowel Shift (see Chapter 1, section 1.3).

In addition to the four principles discussed so far, Ryan briefly mentions a fifth principle, called the *any-spelling principle*, suggesting that written units can indicate meaning without designating sound in any consistent way at all (Ryan, 2018: 84–85). While examples of spelling forms affected by the any-spelling principle are rare in English, they are actually relatively high-frequency words. Among these, *yacht* and *thorough* are notorious examples of words with a complex relationship between letters and sounds, which contribute to making English orthography appear haphazard and unregulated (Ryan, 2018: 85). Other relevant examples are those falling within the category of *ideograms*, symbolic graphic units used in order to refer to concepts in a relatively abstract way (Cook, 2004: 4).[4] Some of the most widely available ideograms in English are § for 'section', $ for 'dollar', € for 'Euro', £ for 'pound', and ⊖, which, in many locations around the world, both English-speaking and not, is used on the road to indicate 'no entry'. Likewise, symbols such as %, which means 'percentage', and @, which indicates the preposition 'at' and is normally found in email addresses, are also ideograms. In register-specific situations, signs used in algebra (+, −, ×, ÷) can also be considered ideograms, as they indicate specific mathematical operations (compare Cook, 2004: 5).

Discussion Material

1. Find six examples in English vocabulary of words where pronunciations are more or less clear (three examples each) on the basis of their spelling forms. Which of the examples you chose are more 'deep' and more 'shallow', and what are the reasons behind their differences?
2. Do you think the spelling rules discussed in section 3.2 are sufficiently systematic for a learner of English as a second language? Motivate your answer.
3. Do you recall any other spelling rules or jingles, in addition to '*i* before *e*, except after *c*', where several exceptions apply? Discuss in class, following the rationale given in section 3.2.

4 However, compare Rogers (2005: 293), who claims that the term 'ideogram' takes many different meanings and should therefore be eschewed, in order to avoid ambiguity.

4. Can you provide additional examples that override the identity principle and show irregularity in the spelling of the same morpheme across different words?
5. Can you think of any word examples where at least three of the four principles of English spelling described in section 3.3 coexist? If not, can you justify your answer?

Recommendations for Reading

Carney, Edward (1994), *A Survey of English Spelling*, London: Routledge, pp. 15–26.

Cook, Vivian (2004), *The English Writing System*, London: Edward Arnold, pp. 56–61.

Crystal, David (2012), *Spell it Out: The Singular Story of English Spelling*, London: St Martin's Press, pp. 175–187.

Ryan, Des (2016), 'Linguists' descriptions of the English writing system', in Vivian Cook and Des Ryan (eds), *The Routledge Handbook of the English Writing System*, London: Routledge, pp. 43–45, 53–58.

Tamošiūnaitė, Aurelija (2023), 'Orthographic conventionality', in Marco Condorelli and Hanna Rutkowska (eds), *The Cambridge Handbook of Historical Orthography*, Cambridge: Cambridge University Press, pp. 82–85.

Part II

Elements

4 Main components

4.1 Some key definitions

The first section of this textbook (Part I) provided contextual information especially relevant to all those wishing to study the English writing system for the first time. The first chapter provided a description of key differences between speech and writing as two different but complementary modes of communication. The second chapter provided a literature review of research in writing system typology and discussed the place of the English writing system in the existing typological frameworks. The third chapter continued the discourse about writing systems by focusing on scholarship describing the English writing system as a relatively complex alphabetic system. The present section (Part II), titled 'Elements', focuses on discussing theoretical terms useful for the study of the English writing system, from *orthography*, *script* and *spelling* to *grapholinguistics*, *graphetics* and *graphematics*. It also describes key components of the English writing system, namely the *graph*, the *glyph* and the *grapheme*, which are the building blocks of English spelling. The focus then moves on to *punctuation* and *capitalisation*, which, according to Rutkowska and Rössler (2012: 214), are at times thought to belong in orthography and at times not.

The shift from a focus on the English writing system as a whole in the first part of the textbook to an emphasis on the individual components within the system in this second part encourages more questions about the use of the words 'orthography', 'script' and 'spelling' in writing system theory. In the first few pages of this textbook, 'orthography' was defined as a term including not only spelling but also additional elements such as punctuation and capitalisation (Coulmas, 1996a: 379–380), which perhaps overly simplifies the statement from Rutkowska and Rössler given above. The reason why disagreements of the likes expressed above exist is that 'orthography' especially is probably the most ambiguous term among those used in writing system research

(Condorelli, 2024: 1). Given these circumstances, let us begin with a focus on the possible meanings applicable to the word 'orthography', delving deeper into some of the points made in the Foreword to this book, and then move on to 'script' and 'spelling'.

The first use of *orthography*, which is polysemous, largely denotes a descriptive approach to studying components of the English writing system (Meletis and Dürscheid, 2022: 171; Condorelli, 2024: 1). In his chapter titled 'Orthography and historical linguistics', for example, Liuzza (1996) describes the grapheme and its complex correlation with the phoneme. In her chapter titled 'Orthography and punctuation', instead, Salmon (1999) offers a descriptive overview of key changes occurring in English spelling, capitalisation and punctuation between 1476 and 1776. The way in which the word 'orthography' is used in the examples above is not only largely analogous to that of 'writing system' but also comparable to the way in which the word is used in non-academic environments to indicate 'spelling' (Condorelli, 2024: 1). Particularly "in everyday usage", Rutkowska writes (2012: 226), "*orthography* is often understood as synonymous [...] with spelling". The polysemous values of the term 'orthography' are also owed to the fact that the word has been subjected to recent theoretical and methodological experimentation in historical linguistics (Condorelli, 2024: 2). In recent years, the words 'historical orthography' have been used to refer to a branch of historical linguistics focused on understanding the historical development of writing systems at different stages of standardisation from a theoretical, methodological and analytical perspective (Condorelli and Rutkowska, 2023: 3–4; Condorelli, 2024: 2).

The second definition of the term 'orthography', which is prescriptive, resonates with the etymological interpretation of the noun. According to the *Oxford English Dictionary*, 'orthography' stems from Latin *orthographia* and Greek *ὀρθογρᾰφῐ́ᾱ*. The latter etymology is, as described in Condorelli (2024: 2), the result of a combination of *ὀρθο-*, 'ortho' for 'correct' and *-γρᾰφῐ́ᾱ*, 'grafia' for 'writing' or 'spelling' (see also Coulmas, 1996a: 379). Stemming from this etymology, the second understanding of 'orthography' is that of a set of prescriptive rules aimed at regulating the ways in which the individual elements of the English writing system (punctuation, capitalisation, spelling) operate, in order to accomplish successful communication. Thus, the original definition of the word places emphasis on the idea that the rules underlying orthography are seen as conventional and are therefore held up as guidelines for everyone to follow (*Oxford English Dictionary*, 'orthography'; Condorelli, 2024: 2). In this sense, 'orthography' is understood as "a normative selection of the possibilities of a script for writing a particular language in a uniform and standardized way" (Coulmas, 1996a: 379). "In the strict sense", Coulmas continues (1996a: 477), "an orthography is a *standardized* spelling system, where the standard has been codified, explicitly in official guidelines, or implicitly through to a tradition developed over the centuries and perhaps laid down in a generally accepted reference work such as a dictionary".

The connection between 'orthography' and the notion of correctness is the reason why the term is highly relevant in sociolinguistic discourse (Condorelli, 2024: 3; see also Chapter 7, section 7.1). As Sebba puts it, "any explanatory account of orthography-as-practice must be sociocultural in nature" (Sebba, 2007: 14). Moreover, "the practices involving literacy in which a community engages are inevitably related to the type of orthography which will emerge as one of the technologies underpinning those practices" (Sebba, 2007: 23–24). The salience of the term 'orthography' in sociolinguistic practice means that the word is also synonymous with the notion of standardisation, in particular by associating the set of principles underling correct orthography with systematic processes of information *encoding* (writing production) and *decoding* (the process of reading, i.e. writing consumption) (Condorelli, 2024: 3).

While more details about orthography and standardisation are covered in Chapter 7 (section 7.1), the sociolinguistic aspect of the word 'orthography' is mentioned here also because of its overlap with that of the word 'script', which is another term affected by the idea of correctness and stylistic encoding (see the differences between roman and black-letter as explained in Chapter 7, section 7.1). The overlap may cause further ambiguity if the word 'script' is not defined as a linguistic term distinct from 'orthography'. In Coulmas' *Blackwell Encyclopedia of Writing Systems* (1996a: 454), *script* is defined as "the graphic form of a writing system", thus encompassing the visual, pragmatic aspect of orthography, spelling, punctuation and capitalisation. This simple definition, however, is followed by a longer explanation, which usefully integrates the explanation provided above:

> In nontechnical contexts the term is often used interchangeably with 'writing system' or 'alphabet', from which it should be distinguished, however. A writing system needs a script for its physical representation, but both are conceptually independent of each other. The same writing system may be written in a variety of scripts. For example, the Roman, Cyrillic, Greek, Russian and runic scripts are different graphic instantiations of the same writing system, the alphabet [...] Scripts, in turn, come

> in different varieties in both handwriting and print, for example the many typefaces that have evolved for the Roman script. (Coulmas, 1996a: 454)[1]

The definition provided by Coulmas, which refers to scripts as "different graphic instantiations of the same writing system", is not to be confused with writer-specific ways of producing letterforms in handwriting. In palaeography, these are known as 'hands' (see Parkes, 1979; further details on palaeography are available in Chapter 7, section 7.1). They are also, as determined in this textbook, not to be confused with typefaces, which, much like hands, may be best understood as subgroups of scripts, in the sense that they offer stylistic varieties for different instantiations of the same writing system. This definition of a script, therefore, differs slightly from that provided by Coulmas above, as a strategy to simplify distinctions between writing styles (e.g. cursive) and scripts (e.g. the Latin script).

In popular discourse, the physical shapes of each letter are not distinguished from the linguistic understanding of the same letters, so that the word 'spelling' is often used for either meaning. In linguistics, however, *spelling* refers to the individual letters (both uppercase and lowercase[2]) that belong to a word (see Coulmas, 1996a: 477–478). Therefore, it most functionally applies to alphabetic systems such as that of English, rather than logographic systems (e.g. Chinese), where logographs are used instead. Since the definition given here for 'spelling' is my own, it is useful to complement it with other definitions, such as that given by the *Oxford English Dictionary*, which describes 'spelling' as follows: "[t]he action, practice, or art of naming the letters of words, of reading letter by letter, or of expressing words by letters". The word is made to derive from the verb 'to spell', which, in the same dictionary, is defined as "[t]o read (a book, etc.) letter by letter; to peruse, or make out, slowly or with difficulty" and "[t]o name or set down in order the letters of (a word or syllable); to enunciate or write letter by letter; to denote by certain letters in a particular order". Given the focus on letters, 'spelling' may be viewed as a subset of 'orthography', especially when this last term is taken to indicate, as explained above, 'all components of the English writing system' or 'a set of norms regulating the English writing system'

1 A typeface is the uniform stylistic layout of a set of characters used for printing. The term is sometimes used interchangeably with *font* (see Gaskell, 1972: 16–33, 283–288).

2 These terms are traditionally used in print for capitalised and non-capitalised letters of the alphabet but have become widely used as synonyms of 'capitalised' and 'non-capitalised'. Their respective counterparts in handwriting are majuscule and minuscule (see Chapter 6, section 6.1).

(Condorelli and Rutkowska, 2023: 3). The relationship between the two terms, and all other terms described in the paragraphs above, is exemplified in Figure 4.1 below (my own diagram). The proportion differences across categories are subjective approximations, aimed at representing the extent of overlapping, frequencies and hierarchical relationships existing among the various components of the English writing system.

While orthography entails the existence of protocols that regulate how to write standardised English, 'spelling' is free from any notion of correctness, unless this idea is conveyed explicitly with auxiliary words (e.g. 'correct spelling'). During most of the medieval era (from c. 450 AD to 1500), spelling arrangements in English were often highly variable, and there was no English orthography (Coulmas, 1996a: 477). An illustrative example is that of *through*, which could be spelled in hundreds of different ways, including *drowgh*, *yhurght*, *trghug* and *trowffe* (examples from Horobin, 2018: 68). The extent of variation existing in the spelling of individual words occurred not only because there was no need for standardisation as we intend it today, but also because variability was appreciated in its own right. As Voeste suggests, "[*v*]*ariatio delectat* [literally, 'variability is pleasing'] meant more than just giving pleasure to the eye. It meant demonstrating one's writing skills through the calculated

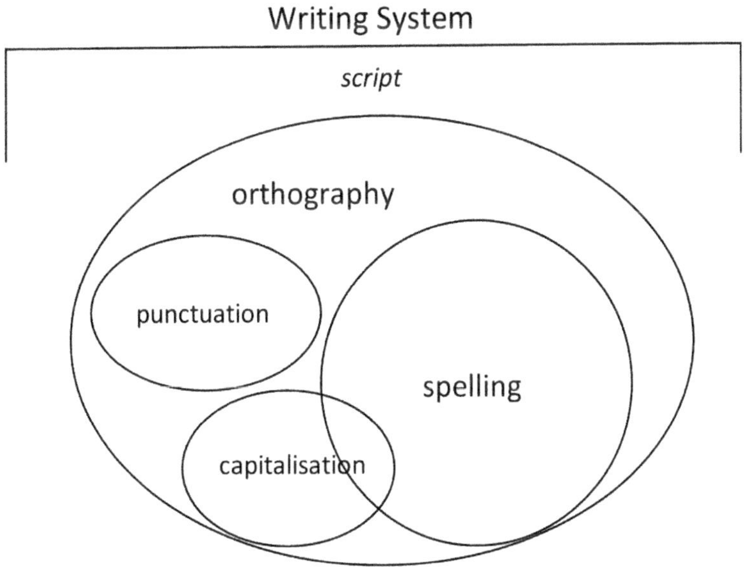

Figure 4.1 Relationship among labels in the English writing system

use of alternation" (Voeste, 2007: 303, also referenced in Rutkowska and Rössler, 2012: 218).

One of the most compelling examples of scholarship mostly focused on English spelling, as opposed to orthography, is Upward and Davidson's *The History of English Spelling* (2011). This book focuses on a chapter-by-chapter descriptive history of each of the twenty-six letters of the Roman alphabet, while also attempting to establish more or less explicit references to English pronunciation. The task undertaken by the book is painstaking, for a couple of reasons. Firstly, a focus on individual letters of the English alphabet means that frequent and detailed references must be made to extinct letters of the English alphabet, such as Old English *thorn*, <þ>, for /θ/ or /ð/ (Upward and Davidson, 2011: 56–58). Secondly, the perspective taken in the book means that the narrative inevitably has to deal with complexities underlying the correlation between spelling and pronunciation. These are evidenced, for example, by the discussion of Old English <e>, which is split into different subheadings, including 'short e', 'long e', 'ea' and 'eo' (Upward and Davidson, 2011: 39–42).

4.2 Graphetics

The definitions established in section 4.1 are essential for a discussion of individual components in the English writing system. A systematic focus on the graph, the glyph, the grapheme, punctuation and capitalisation, in particular, requires rejecting the fluid, polysemous uses of the word 'orthography' discussed in section 4.1, and embracing all the other, more precise distinctions proposed above among 'orthography', 'script' and 'spelling'. The graph, the glyph and the grapheme, in particular, are the main constituents of English spelling, as their respective definitions aim primarily at offering different theoretical perspectives on the individual letters which belong to a word. Punctuation and capitalisation can also be defined within the framework of the graph, the glyph and the grapheme. Like spelling, punctuation and capitalisation can be subjected to English orthography, in the sense that they may be regulated by prescriptive expectations in the same way as spelling may be expected to follow a prescribed standard.

The systematic approach followed in order to distinguish 'spelling' from 'orthography', and the nuances established between 'script' and 'spelling' in section 4.1, are at the heart of two recently established areas of academic enquiry focused on writing system theory, graphetics and graphematics. According to Meletis and Dürscheid (2022: 56), *graphetics* focuses on "the [...] material subsystem of a writing system, consisting of all its graphic resources"; it is, therefore, the knowledge area where elements related to English script as a physical entity (its alphabet and its uniqueness) are studied and described (Coulmas, 1996a: 177–178). *Graphematics*, instead, concerns itself with "how the visual units of writing assume linguistic functions" (Meletis and Dürscheid, 2022: 115), and it is the area which deals with all theoretical information that can be extracted from the practical application of a writing system, its spelling and its orthography (Coulmas, 1996a: 176–177). Among the elements studied in graphetics, the graph and the glyph are especially relevant, while the grapheme, punctuation and capitalisation, discussed in the following sections, are more closely tied to graphematics (compare the approach followed by Hartmann and Szczepaniak, 2023: 50–51). The respective graphetic definitions of the *graph* and the *glyph* are as follows:

- The **graph** is defined as "the smallest formal unit of written language on the level of handwriting or print" (Coulmas, 1996a: 173). According to this definition, all signs existing in the English writing system can be identified as graphs, from uppercase and lowercase letters, to spaces, punctuation marks, numerals, abbreviations and special symbols like *%* and *&*.[3] A simple way to think about graphs in each of the examples mentioned above is that of focusing on the physical realisation of each individual sign. In the word *occurrence*, as printed in each individual copy of this textbook, for instance, there are three separate physical realisations of the letter *c*. In other words, there are three graphs representing the letter *c* (see Meletis and Dürscheid, 2022: 63).
- The **glyph** indicates the different shapes that a punctuation mark or a letter can take when represented visually; when applied to spelling, it signals different possible stylistic variations of a single letter of the alphabet (Hartmann and Szczepaniak, 2023: 65). By using different fonts among those available in a Word document, for example, the letter *c* may be represented in several different glyphs, including, but not limited to, c in Verdana, c in Arial, c in Rockwell and **c** in Rockwell Extra Bold. These glyphs are considered variants of the same letter (the letter *c*) because they have closely comparable shapes and are always found in interchangeable positions in relevant word spellings (compare Haugen, 2013: 100; Hartmann and Szczepaniak, 2023: 66). While the examples of stylistic variation given above are specifically related to printing and machine-mediated typing, the

[3] Graphs are usually not in angle brackets but may sometimes appear in italics (see Condorelli and Rutkowska, 2023: 12).

same principle applies in handwriting, where each person's attempt at writing the letter *c* following a specific style generates a glyph of the same letter (compare the palaeographic definition of 'hand' given in section 4.1).

Departing from the definitions given for the graph and the glyph, one may be tempted to think of graphetics as a field broadly comparable to phonetics, in the sense that it describes actual instances of a linguistic entity rather than its theoretical understanding (Meletis and Dürscheid, 2022: 58). Graphetics, however, is not just "a science of the individual", like phonetics (Catach, 2001: 75, as translated by Meletis and Dürscheid, 2022: 58). It also encourages a focus on "the social and industrial level of writing, which is both a technique and an institution" (Catach, 2001: 75, as translated by Meletis and Dürscheid, 2022: 58). The reason why graphetics is perhaps more socially oriented than phonetics is that, while each person's speech has a virtually unlimited number of idiosyncrasies which can escape analysis, physical written language is, at least in print, limited and more objectively verifiable, and, therefore, can be studied according to shared similarities and differences (Meletis and Dürscheid, 2022: 58–59).

A perspective that allows for comparable graphetic insights is that of *spatial dimension*, the relationship between individual graphic elements and the surface on which they appear. Widths, for example, can be compared between two letters, two words and two paragraphs and, within this hierarchical framework, productive stylistic similarities and differences may be studied across groups of letters appearing in the same printed font or handwriting style. One of the advantages of being able to analyse similarities and differences systematically is the fact that patterns arising from graphetic analyses can be more straightforwardly evaluated in terms of their semiotics.[4]

Mark Sebba's work provides some clear examples of productive connections between writing systems and their semiotics. In *Spelling and Society* (Sebba, 2007), for instance, the author identifies ways in which writing can be seen as having socially relevant functions on various levels, for example the use of theoretically correct, but unusual, conventions for individual word spellings; the application of variant spelling to represent varieties of English; and the use of non-alphabetic characters, such as numbers, where regular spelling is otherwise expected (Sebba, 2007: 34–38). Sebba also provides examples of orthographic

[4] The term 'semiotics' pertains to how the visual aspects of writing convey meaning (see Meletis and Dürscheid, 2022: 59).

issues stemming from social tension, including that of representing 'folk voices' and the extent to which this warrants improved phonetic representations. The author surveys ways to create a more obvious connection with prestigious varieties, or to mark a variety of written English (for example, Jamaican Creole) as different from another one (for instance, Standard American English) (Sebba, 2007: 102–131; see also Chapter 7, section 7.1).

Socio-pragmatic occurrences of the type explained above can be analysed in graphetics following three main routes: productional, descriptive, and perceptual (Meletis and Dürscheid, 2022: 61–62). *Productional* graphetics is concerned with studying aspects related to the making of orthographic elements, from psychological to mechanical processes involved in the process of writing. *Descriptive* graphetics is focused on the structural and systematic classification of individual graphetic features, for example in relation to how individual typographic elements are pragmatically organised. *Perceptual* graphetics deals with issues inherent to the ways in which our senses can absorb, whether consciously or subconsciously, the physical features of writing. Descriptive graphetics may be understood as a subgroup of perceptual graphetics, as the act of describing individual graphetic features occurs through perception (Meletis and Dürscheid, 2022: 61–62).

While Sebba's useful references to some of the levels of socio-pragmatic analysis above (e.g. in studying graffiti) may give the impression that graphetics is a well-known area of research enquiry, its systematic application to the English writing system has actually been relatively scarce. The existing level of underdevelopment and the lack of shared guidelines on graphetic research is probably exacerbated by the recent closure of one of the most important English-language journals on writing-related topics, *Writing Systems Research* (Meletis, 2020a: 128). While the relative state of protocol anarchy in writing system theory is felt especially by scholars and students in English-speaking academic environments, Germany has a long track record in teaching and research practice in writing system theory – some of which is useful for reflecting about components of the English writing system such as those discussed here.

One of the first milestones in the development of a solid modern tradition in writing system theory in Germany was the formation of a research group called *Forschungsgruppe Orthographie* in the 1970s ('Orthography Research Group'). Writing system research in Germany has since grown rapidly and exponentially, reaching important milestones like the publication of *Schrift und Schriftlichkeit/Writing and its Use* (Gunther and Ludwig, 1994–1996), a bulky two-volume compendium of many aspects on the topic (Meletis and Dürscheid, 2022: 3). Other books from the twenty-first-century generation of German scholars who pioneered the modern study of writing system theory include those by Florian Coulmas, which, as evidenced by some of the references made so far, still greatly inform writing system research in English. Particularly relevant examples are *Writing Systems of the World* (Coulmas, 1989), *The Blackwell Encyclopedia of Writing Systems* (Coulmas, 1996a), *Writing Systems: An Introduction to their Linguistic Analysis* (Coulmas, 2002) and *Writing and Society: An Introduction* (Coulmas, 2013).

More recent achievements include the publication of an introductory-level volume on the subject, titled *Einführung in die Schriftlinguistik* ('Introduction to the Linguistics of Writing', Dürscheid, 2016 [2002]), followed by *The Nature of Writing. A Theory of Grapholinguistics* (Meletis, 2020b) and *Writing Systems and their Use: An Overview of Grapholinguistics* (Meletis and Dürscheid, 2022). This last book is especially useful for framing definitions of individual components of the English writing system, since the volume, written in English, represents the only up-to-date summary of current knowledge in grapholinguistics. The term *grapholinguistics* literally means 'the linguistics of writing', and it refers to a linguistic subfield which focuses on the theoretical and material aspects of all writing systems, encompassing both graphetics and graphematics (Neef, 2015: 711). The influence of the German tradition in grapholinguistics on the English community has recently culminated in the establishment of a new book series titled *Grapholinguistics and its Applications*, hosted by Fluxus Editions, and edited by Yannis Haralambous. The book series is home not only to conference proceedings such as those of the *Grapholinguistics in the 21st Century* conference, but also a growing number of English language monographs with a more explicit interest in graphematics.

4.3 Graphematics

The goal of graphematics "is to investigate how the visual units of writing assume linguistic functions (distinguishing the meaning of words, for example) and how they relate to linguistic units such as phonemes and morphemes" (Meletis and Dürscheid, 2022: 115). While the definition provided above makes graphematics ambiguously close to the second, more systematic definition of 'orthography' given earlier in this chapter (a set of prescriptive rules aimed at regulating the ways in which the individual elements of the English writing system operate; see section 4.1), the two can in fact be distinguished clearly. As Barbarić explains (2023: 130), graphematics is concerned with a *descriptive* level of writing system analysis while orthography deals with a *prescriptive* approach to understanding writing systems (see also section 4.1). Meletis and Dürscheid (2022: 117) complement this statement by explaining that the descriptive element of graphematics makes it a *compulsory* constituent of writing systems, while the prescriptive nature of orthography makes it an *optional* component. Referencing Meletis (2020b: 155–159), Barbarić (2023: 130) continues explaining that "[c]ommunication is the most important graphematical function, whereas conventionalization and standardization are most important for orthography".

Among the components studied in graphematics, the *grapheme* is the most central element of descriptive analysis. Its first of two definitions is as follows:

- The **grapheme (definition 1)** has traditionally been understood as the "written representation of a phoneme" (Hartmann and Szczepaniak, 2023: 52). Under this definition, the grapheme functions as a basic contrastive element in the English writing system and can be represented by anything indicating a phoneme – in most cases, a letter of the English alphabet (Rogers, 2005: 10). As an example, Rogers (2005: 10) mentions the grapheme <b> for /b/, which, in English, contrasts with other graphemes, like <p>, <t>, <a>, <l>, <r>, <x>.

The word 'contrastive', in the definition provided above, means not only that it is in opposition to other graphemes in the English writing system, but also that it is a distinct graphic unit. Using the term 'grapheme' is thus a more precise way of identifying distinct graphic units in the English writing system than labels such as *letter*, *character* or *symbol*, which are sometimes used as synonyms of the grapheme or of spelling (Coulmas, 1996a: 72, 291–292; Rogers, 2005: 294, 298; Hartmann and Szczepaniak, 2023: 56). The term *letter*, among these synonyms, is one with a great deal of historical significance, as it was used, in antiquity, to indicate sounds and written graphic units indiscriminately (Rutkowska, 2012: 229). As described in Rutkowska (2012: 229, referencing Abercrombie, 1981 [1949]: 14, and Henderson, 1985: 142), the term indicated, in antiquity, "the smallest element of language, combining three attributes, *nomen* (name used for identification), *figura* (shape or visual configuration), and *potestas* (power to signify sound)". The use of the word 'letter' as a synonym of the term 'grapheme', under the first grapheme definition given here, is therefore historically derived.

While the example of <b> for /b/ given in the bullet point definition above is relatively simple, graphemes identified under the first definition are not always one-letter units, as the identification of phonemes is sometimes complicated, as discussed in Chapters 2 and 3, by the irregular correlation between letters and sounds in English. "Distinctive contrasts" (Rogers, 2005: 16) available in speech may not be found in writing and vice versa, which is the reason why English vocabulary has *homographic* words, where the spelling forms are the same but sounds are different, and *homophonous* words, where pronunciations are the same but the spelling forms are different, such as those described in Chapter 2 and 3. One of the more complex forms in which graphemes may appear is that of a *digraph*: <sh>, for instance, is a two-letter grapheme indicating one sound, namely /ʃ/ as in *shower* (Rogers, 2005: 16, 292). Another example is that of the digraph <th>, which, as briefly seen in Chapter 3 (section 3.2), may represent different sounds depending on word context (*teeth* vs. *either* vs. *Thames*, pronounced, respectively, /tiːθ/, British English /aɪðə/ and /temz/) (Rogers, 2005: 17).

While digraphs are common, the English writing system also uses *trigraphs*, which occur when three individual letters are grouped together in order to signify one sound (Coulmas, 1996a: 512). An example of a trigraph, which, under the definition given above, would be considered a grapheme, is that of <igh>, which indicates the diphthong /aɪ/ in words such as *night* and *flight*. The inconsistent relationship between phonemes and letters may also result in a *polyphone*, which occurs when a grapheme indicates two or more separate sounds, pronounced consecutively as one unit (Rogers, 2005: 16). Polyphones are rare in English, but one example still available today is that of the grapheme <x>, which stands for the two sounds /ks/ in words like *excuse* and *sexy* (Rogers, 2005: 16).

To account for the fact that different individual letters of the alphabet may indicate the same phoneme, the phonological definition of the grapheme also requires the existence of a graphematic unit of analysis that expresses a non-contrastive linguistic function: the *allograph* (the use of the expression 'non-contrastive' here echoes Rogers, 2005: 10). Uppercase and lowercase letters are frequently understood, under the definition of the grapheme given above, as allographs, as their alternation takes a grammatical, rather than a phonological function (Coulmas, 1996a: 173–174). Thus, for example, when uppercase *A* for /æ/ occurs to signal the beginning of a new sentence, lowercase *a* may occur in the same sentence indicating exactly the same sound. On many occasions, the allograph does not change the meaning of a word, so that the word *Another* is semantically identical to *another* (Coulmas, 1996a: 173; see Chapter 6, section 6.1 for further details on free allography).

At this point, one may wonder whether a neat theoretical demarcation can be made between the allograph and the glyph (described in section 4.2). The difference between the two is indeed subtle: while the glyph is a graphetic definition and, therefore, is linguistically independent, the allograph is a graphematic one and is more closely connected to its correspondent grapheme (compare Hartmann and Szczepaniak, 2023: 64). Thus, the glyph and the allograph are distinguished by a material vs. a linguistic interpretation of the same type of variation (see Coulmas, 1996a: 9, 168; Hartmann and Szczepaniak, 2023: 56–58, 64–66; Barbarić, 2023: 131–132).

Let us now take a step back and return to discussing graphematic definitions of the grapheme, since only one of the two possible definitions has so far been examined. The second definition of the grapheme arises from the argument that, when the grapheme is considered to be analogical to the phoneme as a way to define it, there appears to be no rationale for distinguishing the grapheme from the phoneme itself. Rather, the grapheme and the phoneme are seen as two components of the same theoretical construction, which means that the grapheme may become superfluous (Günther, 1988: 76; Barbarić, 2023: 131). For this reason, the second definition of the grapheme is sometimes used as a way of correcting the first definition, expressing the idea that the grapheme is not a phoneme but rather it may be *parallel* to it (Barbarić, 2023: 131). The resulting definition is as follows:

- The **grapheme (definition 2)** is defined as "the unit of analysis in the study of written language understood as an abstract entity" (Coulmas, 1996a: 174). It is also defined as "the smallest functional unit of writing on whatever structural level of language the writing system operates" (Coulmas, 1996a: 174). Similarly, Hartmann and Szczepaniak (2023: 52) suggest that the grapheme may be intended as "a minimal contrastive unit in a writing system" and "a letter". In an alphabetic writing system like that of English, graphemes typically correspond to individual letters of the alphabet, though diacritic marks such as accents and punctuation marks such as commas may also be considered graphemes.

Under both definitions provided above, the grapheme may be intended to be either free or bound: a *free grapheme* is a grapheme that occurs without constraints on position and graphic context, while a *bound grapheme* is restricted to appearing only in combination with another grapheme (Rogers, 2005: 11). Examples of free graphemes are common in English, and include, for example, <a>, <b>, <c>, <d>, <e>, covering the full English alphabet. Examples of bound graphemes, instead, are fewer, and include units such as <é> in *cliché*, where the acute accent <´>, also a grapheme by the second definition provided above (see also Chapter 5, section 5.1, with reference to diacritics), appears in combination with <e>.

Bound graphemes are not to be confused with *ligatures*, which occur when two graphemes appear as visually, rather than functionally, joined (Rogers, 2005: 12). In most cases, ligatures in English do not have any distinctive value and are only used for visual purposes. An example given by Rogers (2005: 12) is that of the units <fi> and <fl>, which, in printed English, often appear as joined due to the fact that the space available between the two letters, in the context of fonts like Times New Roman, is too little to allow for sufficient separation between them. Ligatures are mostly discussed in graphetics rather than graphematics, but there are exceptions where ligatures overlap between the two areas. An example is that of the ampersand <&>, which stems from Latin *et*, meaning 'and' (see Rosen, 2015: 296), and while being a ligature of <e> and <t>, it is sometimes considered to be a stand-alone grapheme (Coulmas, 1996a: 295). While present-day English only features the ampersand as an example of a special ligature, Old English featured a ligature which worked as an individual grapheme distinct from its two parent graphemes: the letter *ash*, represented by <æ>, was a blend between the graphemes <a> and <e> (Upward and Davidson, 2011: 23–24; Coulmas, 1996a: 295).

Whether the graphemes are free or bound, there exist regulations governing the way in which grapheme combinations manifest within individual word contexts. In graphematics, the concept of *graphotactics* refers to such regulations. Graphotactic constraints give limitations on how written elements organise themselves both in relation to each other and hierarchically within the English writing system, from the smallest to the largest linguistic segments (McCawley, 1994: 115; Meletis and Dürscheid, 2022: 148). Graphotactic constraints are dependent on phonology and morphology, so that some of the ways in which graphic units in the English writing system work as a system follow sound-based and lexeme-based criteria ('what sound combinations are possible in English and what combinations are prohibited, and how do these interrelate with the consistent representation of morphemes?'). An example cited in Meletis and Dürscheid (2022: 148, following McCawley, 1994: 117) to illustrate this point is that of the fact that <v> almost never occurs word-finally in English; instead, this grapheme is almost always followed by <e>.

Another graphotactic constraint in English is that involving the repetition of some graphemes, for example <jj> and <ww>, which are not allowed in English (see Berg and Evertz, 2018: 193; see also Meletis and Dürscheid, 2022: 149). Graphotactic constraints also apply to English punctuation, and they dictate where and how in the sentence punctuation marks may be found. Graphotactic constraints are not to be intended as regulations akin to those followed to establish correct English orthography. Instead, they form an integral aspect of the structure inherent in the English writing system, working on the basis of expected assumption from individuals engaging with it (Meletis and Dürscheid, 2022: 148). The boundaries between graphotactics and orthographic rules, however, are sometimes blurred, so that constraints existing in graphotactics may be seen as informing English orthography. Graphotactic principles have changed over time, and historical English has some interesting examples of graphotactic constraints which do not apply today. According to Tamošiūnaitė (2023: 86), the groups <i>, <j>, <y> and <u>, <v> are among the most frequently occurring examples of graphotactically regulated graphemes between the sixteenth and the seventeenth centuries.

Word-initial <u>/<v> and <i>/<j> in English (discussed in Condorelli, 2021a) underwent some remarkable changes between 1500 and 1700. The grapheme <v> often appeared word-initially, as in *vntil*, while <u> was found in all other positions, e.g. in *loue*. The grapheme <j> was an allograph of <i>, and was found in Latin numbers such as *iiij* for '4', while <i> was available in all other places, for example in *iudge*. During the seventeenth century, <v> and <j> began to take mostly word-initial positions, indicating, respectively, /v/ and /dʒ/, while <u> and <i> were found elsewhere. The grapheme <u> signified /ju:/, /ʌ/ and /ʊ/, e.g. in *due*, *cut* and *bull*, while <i> indicated /ɪ/ and /eɪ/, e.g. in *ship* and *time* (examples from Condorelli, 2021a: 799; see also Chapter 7, sections 7.1 and 7.2, for a more extensive discussion of the history of <i>/<j>).

The graphemes <i> and <y> (discussed in Condorelli, 2021b) also followed different graphotactic constraints from those available in present-day English. Between 1500 and 1700, their appearance was regulated both by letter position within individual words and by word class. From the early sixteenth-century, the grapheme <i> in word-initial position normally indicated a vowel, as in *iron* and *intent*, while word-initial <y> indicated a glide, as in *year* and *young*. In word-final position, <ye>, <y> and <ie> were used as allographs, for example in words like *praye*, *city* and *duetie* (examples from Condorelli, 2021b: 101–102). During the mid-sixteenth century, <ye> and <ie> were supplanted by <y> word-finally. At around the same time, word-medial <i> and <y> went from following a lexical distribution, whereby <i> was present in function words, such as *this* and *with*, while <y> was used in content words, to a new arrangement, where <i> was used across most word-medial contexts and <y> in all other positions described above.

Discussion Material

1. How did you use the word 'orthography' before reading section 4.1?
2. Are there any strategies that are worth implementing within and across universities to support the theoretical study of the English writing system in academia?
3. How do graphetics and graphematics intersect and complement each other to give us a fuller understanding of the English writing system? Discuss in class, drawing on examples given in this chapter or providing your own.
4. Scholarly debates about the *graph*, the *glyph* and the *grapheme* are sometimes more complex than has been shown in this chapter. Look up their individual definitions in Hartmann and Szczepaniak (2023) and discuss in class their similarities and differences.
5. Provide additional examples of graphotactic constraints in English. Which do you think are driven by phonological/morphological reasons and which are not? What is the reason behind the existence of any examples that follow rules outside the remits of phonology and morphology?

Recommendations for Reading

Condorelli, Marco (2021a), 'Positional spelling redistribution: Word-initial <u>/<v> and <i>/<j> in Early Modern English (1500–1700)', *English Language and Linguistics* 25 (4), pp. 799–823.

Condorelli, Marco (2021b), 'The standardisation of *i* and *y* in Early Modern English (1500–1700)', *English Studies* 102 (1), pp. 101–123.

Hartmann, Stefan and Renata Szczepaniak (2023), 'Elements of writing systems', in Marco Condorelli and Hanna Rutkowska (eds), *The Cambridge Handbook of Historical Orthography*, Cambridge: Cambridge University Press, pp. 50–73.

Meletis, Dimitrios and Christa Dürscheid (2022), *Writing Systems and their Use: An Overview of Grapholinguistics*, Berlin and Boston: De Gruyter Mouton, pp. 56–114, 115–168.

Rogers, Henry (2005), *Writing Systems: A Linguistic Approach*, Malden and Oxford: Blackwell Publishing, pp. 10–12, 16–17.

5 Punctuation

5.1 Defining punctuation

The previous chapter gave a brief introduction to graphetics and graphematics, describing their role in defining elements within the English writing system. Graphetics was introduced as a subfield in grapholinguistics dealing with the physical aspects of the English writing system; graphematics, instead, as an area focusing on the linguistic purposes of the graphic units available in the English writing system. This chapter continues the graphematic discussion of components in the English writing system by focusing on punctuation, which plays a central role in providing written English with clarity and order. The term *punctuation* refers to all those written signs used in order to structure written English and help the reader with understanding its meaning (Coulmas, 1996a: 421). While punctuation may be a relatively straightforward orthographic category for the average reader, the graphematic understanding of punctuation is not as simple a matter as it may be for other elements of the English writing system.

Although punctuation marks generally do not have sound values in spoken English, and cannot therefore count as graphemes under the first grapheme definition given in Chapter 4 (section 4.3), they still frequently have contrastive value; in other words, they can act as distinct graphic units in English orthography (compare the second definition of the grapheme given in Chapter 4, section 4.3). Unlike spelling, the contrastive value of punctuation is not on the word level, but rather on the syntactic and, consequentially, on the semantic levels (Meletis and Dürscheid, 2022: 142). Compare the following sentences, which have become common-knowledge examples on the internet, as a way of illustrating how the absence or the presence of punctuation, in alternation, radically changes meanings by affording syntactic reinterpretations of the same sentence: *I find inspiration in cooking my family and my dog* / *I find inspiration in cooking, my family, and my dog.* And this other example:

Employees wash your hands before returning to work / *Employees: wash your hands before returning to work!* And, finally: *He played in all three games* / *He played, in all, three games.*

In the first of the three sentences given above, the person speaking might either be assumed, depending on punctuation, to cook their family and their dog as part of their meal recipe, or to find inspiration in three different, separate elements, namely cooking, their family and their pet dog. Likewise, in the second example, punctuation is the only difference between stating that a number of employees take up the task of washing your hands before returning to work and instructing all employees to wash their hands before returning to work. Similarly, the third example could either mean that a person played in each of all three games organised or that they played, in total, three games out of however many games were played. In all three examples, punctuation acts in a way that is somewhat similar to how two sounds distinguish two different meanings in a word (e.g. *chair* vs. *pair*): in other words, it becomes the basis for a 'minimal pair'. Although the example given here is chiefly grammatical, there is still some tension, today, between the structural and the prosodic interpretation of punctuation. In particular, it may be argued that punctuation also has a strong influence on giving written sentences shades of meaning that might otherwise not be possible. Examples that, once again, have become common knowledge on the internet include the use of the question mark in sentences where the question is rhetorical rather than a genuine attempt to seek an answer, which means that the question has a different intonation from that of a traditional question; or the use of three dots at the end of a sentence to slow down the pace of reading, while also signalling that the sentence is grammatically incomplete. The rhetorical aspect of punctuation stems from the fact that reading in silence is often perceived as 'reading as hearing', which occurs through an internalised voice that follows prosodic reading as if it were a speaker, or indeed the voice of the narrator (Jajdelska, 2007: 8–9).

While defining the role and importance of punctuation in English written communication is still a relatively easy task, an even more difficult aspect of punctuation is that of picking out its components: which graphic units belong to the category of punctuation? In keeping with the remarks on the development of grapholinguistics made in Chapter 4 (section 4.2), tentative answers to the question posed above mostly stem from theoretical contributions made by German scholars over the last two decades. While German scholars' observations were made making reference to the German writing system, most of their insights, as evidenced by the discussion made in Chapter 4 and this chapter (section 5.1), can also be carried over to the English writing system, since both German and English use the Roman alphabet.[1] For some scholars (e.g. Müller, 1964; Nunberg et al., 2002; Carter and McCarthy, 2006), 'punctuation' is understood rather permissively, with an inventory encompassing a wide range of graphic signs. It includes, for example, blank spaces and line breaks, boldface and italics, and even capitalisation (Hartmann and Szczepaniak, 2023: 67; Kirchhoff and Primus, 2016: 93). This permissive understanding of punctuation also encompasses diacritics such as accents,[2] which, as discussed in Chapter 4 (section 4.3), are added to individual letters as part of the overall orthographic form of an individual word (Coulmas, 1996a: 126–127).

While accents generally have the purpose of indicating stress, some diacritic marks are found in English only as remnants of their foreign etymological origins. Examples in English vocabulary are mostly from French, and entail the use of the diaeresis in *Chloë* (in addition to *naïve*, mentioned in the Foreword), the acute accent in *résumé*, the circumflex accent in the word *pâté*, and the cedilla in *façade* (compare Rogers, 2005: 161).[3] In English dictionaries, letters containing diacritics are still normally considered as a separate category from letters without any diacritics, so that, for example, words beginning with an accented letter follow words beginning with the same non-accented letter. It is possible, however, to encounter the words above written without their original diacritic marks, as all non-accented variants are non-contrastive (see Bennett, 2015 for further details).

As an alternative to the permissive understanding of punctuation, recent years have seen other scholars, especially Bredel (2008, 2011), arguing for a more restrictive definition. Bredel's restrictive definition is best summarised by Kirchhoff and Primus (2016: 94): punctuation consists of "segmental units that are identifiable without other signs, not recordable by audible spoken units, not freely combinable with each other and not paired in lowercase and uppercase variants". The advantage of this definition, which is the reason why Bredel's approach has become so popular in grapholinguistics, is that it helps to create a marked separation between punctuation and traditional graphemes.

1 Statements made in section 5.1 are contextualised by providing English-language examples, in the footsteps of Kirchhoff and Primus' chapter on punctuation available in the *Routledge Handbook of the English Writing System* (2016).

2 A subcategory of diacritics, which includes, for example, <´> and <`> (acute and grave), is commonly known as *accents*.

3 These and other examples are available on Wikipedia (<https://en.wikipedia.org/wiki/English_terms_with_diacritical_marks> [accessed September 2025]). Note Wikipedia's adjectival use 'diacritical' for the noun 'diacritic'.

As further detailed by Meletis and Dürscheid (2022: 143–144), the conditions that create a departure of punctuation from our understanding of graphemes are as follows:

1. Punctuation should be visible in a context-free environment; this rule inevitably excludes the blank space, which can exist only when other graphic marks are available in its vicinity.
2. It should not be verbalised; this criterion rules out the <&> sign, which can be read as ‘and’, and all alphabet-derived graphemes, such as <p>, which can be pronounced as /p/.
3. It should not be joined with other punctuation marks; this option excludes, for example, digits, such as <21>, which can appear together.
4. It should not have capitalised and non-capitalised variants, as units in the English alphabet do.

These four points address both of the questions raised in this chapter so far – whether we can consider punctuation marks as graphemes, and what exactly should be intended by punctuation. According to Bredel (2008, 2011), the inventory resulting from the restrictions above includes, in order of relative frequency on an average text, the following items: , . … - – : ; ’ “ ” ? ! ( ). Each of these punctuation marks has traditionally been assigned specific linguistic functions in written English (compare the relevant entries available in Coulmas, 1996a).[4] The basic graphematic functions of the individual punctuation marks identified above are as follows:

- The **comma** is generally used as a tool for enhancing semantic clarity and is a solution for joining or splitting clauses (*Oxford English Dictionary*, ‘comma’). One peculiar use of this punctuation mark in English is that of the so called ‘Oxford comma’, where the comma immediately precedes the final conjunction, for instance in *I enjoyed watching the ghost hunting show, hearing the soundtracks, and meeting the crew.* Commas can also have the purpose of signalling an interjection, for instance in *The student, said the teacher, was a history enthusiast.*
- Unlike the comma, the **full stop** is generally found at the end of a sentence (e.g. *Sarah won the prize.*), or next to a capitalised letter to signal a type of abbreviation called *initialism* or *acronym* (see the

[4] See also the University of Lynchburg’s *A Quick Guide to Punctuation*, which has informed several of the individual graphematic functions and has inspired some relevant examples in the following paragraphs (<www.lynchburg.edu/academics/writing-center/wilmer-writing-center-online-writing-lab/grammar/a-quick-guide-to-punctuation/> [accessed January 2025]).

distinction between the two made below), for example in *U.S.A.* (*Oxford English Dictionary*, 'full stop', 'period'). The use of the full stop to signal initialisms is becoming less frequent, but it is still found in a few examples, including *Abbr.* for 'abbreviation' and *St.* for 'street'. There are other uses of the full stop where frequency has not declined at all. One of these is when the full stop is used as a decimal separator, in which case it is called a *point* (e.g. *£11.50*), whereas in internet-mediated communication it is normally referred to as a dot (e.g. in *gmail.com*).

- Although it does not appear as frequently as the full stop, the **ellipsis** is a derivate of the full stop. It consists in the repetition of the full stop (normally totalling three dots) to indicate that a portion of text has been omitted, especially within square brackets (*Oxford English Dictionary*, 'ellipsis'). For instance, *As Sam mentioned in his book, "education is key for wisdom [...] and emancipation"*. It may also be used to give the idea that the number of items listed in a sentence is not complete or to convey a sense of impending danger. An example of the latter would be as follows: *The Robinsons were delighted to move to the new mansion. Little did they know, however, that something sinister lurked within those walls ...*
- The hyphen and the dash are two closely interrelated punctuation marks, in the sense that they visually look similar, but cover slightly different functions. **Hyphens** are normally used in order to merge together compound words (*Oxford English Dictionary*, 'hyphen'). Examples include *short-term*, *full-scale*, *self-imposed*, *six-pack*, *deep-fried*, and so on. Hyphens also have a strong correlation with line-final word division (also known as 'word separation', see Coulmas, 1996a: 550–551), a process where individual words are split apart, most frequently at the end of a line (examples available on most pages of this textbook). While most of the principles behind this process are now automated when we write on digital documents, the internet is rife with guidelines on line-final word division in handwriting with conservative instructions (along the lines of 'as a first step, consider if you really need to split a word into two halves for space issues'), alongside linguistically unreliable suggestions (for example, 'always split words in natural ways').
- The **dash** is usually not as frequent as the hyphen, as it indicates a digression. Dashes are identifiable in two subtypes, the **en-dash** and the **em-dash** (*Oxford English Dictionary*, 'en dash', 'em dash'). The only visible difference between the en-dash and the em-dash is their length: the former is shorter, the latter is longer. An example sentence using the en-dash is: *Please read pages 15–20 for further*

information. An example sentence using the em-dash is *Josh couldn't believe it — he had finally gotten his dream job.* Sometimes, the dash can take the place of a comma, a colon or a semicolon (e.g. *Her hobbies, making poetry and reading novels, gave her comfort* vs. *Her hobbies — making poetry and reading novels — gave her comfort*). If the text where the dash appears permits it, it is a matter of style and personal choice whether dashes or commas, colons and semicolons, or all of the above in alternation, are used.

- The **colon** is usually used to make an assertion that further qualifies a preceding sentence (*Oxford English Dictionary*, 'colon'). The clause on the immediately right-hand side of the colon generally adds to or illustrates something that precedes the colon itself. A typical grammatical use of the colon is when it is followed by a statement with an independent subject and a verb. For instance, *Mark's envisaged lifestyle was simple: he wanted to live in the countryside and farm his own food.* However, there are also instances where the colon is used in order to introduce a list of items or names. For example, in *The following applicants were successful: Mark Mendez, Rose Lawrence and Kassi McAllister.*
- Unlike the colon, where one sentence is somewhat dependent on the other, the **semicolon** is normally used to juxtapose two or more main clauses with closely related meanings (*Oxford English Dictionary*, 'semicolon'). While the two clauses may have the most varied structure and semantic content, there are often signalling words that follow a semicolon, such as *instead*, *however*, *admittedly*, *truthfully*, *additionally*, and so on. An example includes *The task was difficult; however, the sense of accomplishment upon completion was rewarding.*
- The **apostrophe** generally has two functions: to indicate ownership and to signal an elision, for example in *John's bike was brand new* and *It's a lovely day today, isn't it?* (*Oxford English Dictionary*, 'apostrophe'). A punctuation mark visually identical to the apostrophe (depending on the font used) is the **single quotation** mark, which, when used in pairs, helps to identify quotations. Single quotation marks are sometimes used interchangeably with **double quotation marks** in order to report speech or to quote something from a different source (*Oxford English Dictionary*, 'quotation marks'). For example, *Anthony said, "I'll see you at school tomorrow"* and *The article stated, '2025 is going to be the hottest year ever recorded.'* Quotation marks are also attached to a word used inappropriately or out of context, in order to show that that word requires exceptional consideration. For instance, *The so-called 'doctor' failed to find an efficient cure for his cold.* A useful functional difference between single and double quotation marks is when a quote within a quote is given: in cases like this, the two

embedded quotes are generally assigned different types of quotation marks, in order to avoid confusion. For instance, *The teacher said "Read Shakespeare's 'Romeo and Juliet' by the end of next week."*

- The **question** and **exclamation marks** are often used in order to indicate sentences in which the speaker/writer expresses, respectively, sentiments of doubt and emphasis (e.g. surprise or excitement) (*Oxford English Dictionary*, 'exclamation mark', 'question mark'). For example, *Are you sure?* and *I can't believe he's wrong!* Exclamation marks are normally not found in essays, and questions marks are rare, although not impossible to find.
- Parentheses, commonly called **round brackets**, can appear both in formal and informal writing styles. The purpose of this category of punctuation marks is to provide details that are deemed peripheral to the overall meaning of the main sentence, especially when it does not fit within the normal syntactic flow of the main clause (*Oxford English Dictionary*, 'parentheses', 'round brackets'). For example: *He eventually reached his destination (after a number of wrong turns) and was glad to find a parking spot.*[5]

According to Bredel (2008, 2011), a useful framework for reviewing the various functions of punctuation marks, as described above, is to categorise them based on their visual aspects. Bredel's alternative approach to punctuation provides a compelling example of how the graphetic level of punctuation (the material, visual aspect of each individual graphic sign) can inform the graphematic level (their linguistic function) and guide the reading process (see Kirchhoff and Primus, 2016: 95; Meletis and Dürscheid, 2022: 144; Hartmann and Szczepaniak, 2023: 68–69). In particular, two major subcategories were identified as applicable to the entire punctuation inventory discussed above, namely clitics and fillers. *Clitics* are punctuation marks that more obviously appear as functionally attached to other graphemes. *Fillers*, instead, take their own independent space and normally connect linguistic units of the same category.

[5] While they are not formally acknowledged by Bredel (2008, 2011), square brackets and curly brackets are also used in English, albeit rarely. Square brackets may be found in situations where, especially within a citation, the writer feels the need to add or skip additional information that is not found in the original sentences. The same example given in the ellipsis paragraph applies for illustrative purposes, as square brackets are frequently used to enclose the ellipsis. Curly brackets are very rare in English and may help to visually identify subcategories, for example in *I bought the ingredients, including pasta, spices {including oregano and basil} and tomato sauce.* See the University of Lynchburg's *A Quick Guide to Punctuation* (<www.lynchburg.edu/academics/writing-center/wilmer-writing-center-online-writing-lab/grammar/a-quick-guide-to-punctuation/> [accessed January 2025]).

On the basis of these criteria, ( ) “ ” . , ; : ? ! are clitics and … – -’ are fillers (Kirchhoff and Primus, 2016: 95–96; Meletis and Dürscheid, 2022: 144).

The two groups play two different roles during the act of reading: fillers aid the process of understanding individual textual features, a process which Bredel calls *scanning*, while clitics help with understanding and connecting overall sentences and other chunks of meaning, which Bredel calls *processing* (Meletis and Dürscheid, 2022: 145–146). Hyphens, for example, aid readers in the process of identifying words visually joined together in structure and meaning. The comma, instead, allows one to go beyond the clause boundaries that it delimits and to connect a finished clause with the following one (Kirchhoff and Primus, 2016: 95–96; Meletis and Dürscheid, 2022: 145–146).

Within the fillers and clitics categories, Bredel (2008, 2011) identifies two visual parameters, which allow for an even more systematic understanding of some of the same graphematic functions identified above. The ‘reduplication’ parameter distinguishes fillers that result from the duplication of a smaller punctuation mark, for example the em-dash being the result of hyphen duplication (Kirchhoff and Primus, 2016: 95). Reduplicated punctuation marks guide the reader “above word level”, while non-reduplicated marks aid “at word level” (Kirchhoff and Primus, 2016: 96; see also Meletis and Dürscheid, 2022: 145). The ‘vertical’ parameter, instead, allows for a classification of punctuation according to whether the individual signs take the upper space of an average textual line or whether they occupy the middle-to-low space. The marks ! ? “ ” ( ) ’ belong to the first group (stretching to the upper space of the line) while the marks : ; . , … - – belong to the second group (occupying the remaining space) (Kirchhoff and Primus, 2016: 95). Vertical punctuation marks aid with the communicative level, for example whenever quotation marks are used to indicate a part of speech that does not belong to the person writing the sentence (e.g. in *‘Let’s go get some food’, Mark said*) (Kirchhoff and Primus, 2016: 96; Meletis and Dürscheid, 2022: 145; Hartmann and Szczepaniak, 2023: 68–69). Non-vertical punctuation marks, instead, signal syntactic parsing, for example when a full sentence is complete and another one begins (e.g. in *He had his eyes set on the prize. Everybody wanted the golden cup.*) (Kirchhoff and Primus, 2016: 96–97; Meletis and Dürscheid, 2022: 145; Hartmann and Szczepaniak, 2023: 68–69).

5.2 Development of punctuation

As evidenced by the definition given in section 5.1, the linguistic understanding of English punctuation today is based on the idea that it has a strongly *syntactic* function; that is to say, it helps with the structural organisation of written English. In the past, however, punctuation was seen as mainly having a *prosodic* function; in other words, it was frequently thought of as an aid for interpreting how sentences would be produced in speech (compare Meletis and Dürscheid, 2022: 142). In between these two chronological milestones, the two approaches often coexisted in the use of each individual punctuation mark. The full stop is a pertinent example: prosodically, this mark was taken to indicate a pause after a sentence; syntactically, it was understood as marking the boundaries between a sentence and another. The development from prosody to syntax as underlying principles regulating the use of punctuation has its roots in the gradual shift, during the course of history, from a culture primarily based on oral reading to one founded on silent reading. The word 'primarily', as used in the previous sentence, is key for understanding how such development occurred: silent reading was known in ancient history, but reading aloud was simply more prevalent and, therefore, it was considered to be the norm (Jajdelska, 2007: 4–5).

As evidenced by an intriguing episode narrated in Augustine's *Confessions* (6.3.3 [2017 translation]), those who chose not to read aloud in antiquity aroused observers' curiosity. Augustine of Hippo (354–430 AD), a widely respected theologian and philosopher, considered to be one of the most important fathers of the Latin Church, made a remark in his autobiographical work about his master Ambrose reading quietly. What surprised Augustine was not so much the fact that the meaning of the text that Ambrose was reading flowed from his master's eyes directly to his mind (i.e. the act of silent reading in its own right), but rather that Ambrose chose to read silently despite the fact that he was frequently visited by a lot of uneducated people. Augustine could simply not make sense of his master's apparently conscious decision to keep knowledge to himself, although he eventually concluded that Ambrose did so to preserve his tired, delicate voice (see Jajdelska, 2007: 5).

While texts were frequently read aloud in antiquity, punctuation was sometimes informally present in the form of mark-up material, as a studying aid for pupils; even when a text served purely oratory purposes, it would have sometimes been punctuated, usually in exquisitely idiosyncratic ways, by the speaker, to help with delivery. One of the earliest, more formal, examples of punctuation in English, however, is available in the Thornhill Fragments, found in the Church of St Michael (near Dewsbury, Yorkshire), consisting of pieces from sandstone crosses with three examples of runic inscriptions carved on them (Elliott, 1963: 87). The most remarkable of the three examples (Fragment C) dates back to the period between the end of the eighth and the first half of the ninth centuries AD (Elliott, 1963: 89). The runes show that the engraver felt the need to use two different types of punctuation, a dot (·) and a colon (:), the former indicating the end of a word and the end of a metrical verse, the latter simply demarcating word boundaries (Elliott, 1963: 88). Here, punctuation was most likely needed to help readers make sense of the characters etched tightly onto small stone surfaces like that of Fragment C.

A more systematic use of punctuation as an aid for silent reading was seen for the first time in the practice of Latin manuscript production of early Irish and Anglo-Saxon scribes from the mid-sixth century onwards. These scribes began to separate words in texts such as the *Cathach of St Columba* (Dublin, Royal Irish Academy, s.n., late sixth century) using blank spaces not so much for literary finesse but because of their lack of familiarity with Latin, which prevented them from reading it silently in continuous writing without incurring major word-recognition difficulties (Parkes, 1992 [2016]: 24–26). Early scribes also began to use the *positura*, a 7-shaped sign which acted as a means to mark the end of a section, and which allowed readers to segment the text into easily digestible chunks (see Parkes, 1992 [2016]: 22).

In France, the court of Charlemagne (747–814 AD) witnessed the rise of a number of punctuation marks that were different from those experimented with by Irish and Anglo-Saxon scribes (in turn, inspired by the Romans), while blank spaces became a staple of Carolingian text structuring (Saenger, 1997: 107). The novelties stemmed from attempts to guide singers in modulating their voice while engaging with liturgical chants, following a musical notation system called *neumes*. According to Parkes (1992 [2016]: 35–36), there were at least four main *positurae* (a revisited medieval term to indicate neumes-derived punctuation) arising from the musical notation system mentioned above: these were the *punctus versus* (;), the *punctus interrogativus* (?), the *punctus elevatus* (:) and the *punctus flexus* (:).[6] The *punctus versus* was used to mark the end of a full sentence, where meaning was complete; the *punctus interrogativus* also marked the end of a full sentence, while also signalling a rising tone such as that of a question; the *punctus elevatus* marked a medial pause when a sentence was not yet finished but there was a point of resolution in terms of meaning; and the *punctus flexus* was used to signpost a smaller pause where neither the meaning nor the sentence

[6] My own drawings, based on Parkes (1992 [2016]: 36), to be intended as approximations.

were yet complete (Parkes, 1992 [2016]: 36). Syntax and prosody went closely together.

The scholar who had initially acknowledged the need to revise punctuation, Alcuin of York (d. 809), had been hired from an English monastery by Charlemagne. While the use of *positurae* spread out across different texts during much of the Middle Ages, these signs coexisted with the system of Latin *distinctiones* deriving from classical antiquity. This system consisted in using the dot at three different heights to indicate pauses of different values. The low dot (*subdistinctio*), frequently recurring where the meaning of a sentence was not yet complete, indicated a short pause; the middle dot (*media distinctio*), normally occurring when the sense was finished but not the meaning, represented a longer pause; and the higher dot (*distinctio*), usually found when the meaning of a sentence was complete, indicated a major pause (Parkes, 1992 [2016]: 13). The two systems worked well in symbiosis: *positurae* sometimes conveniently integrated *distinctiones* in their ability to provide guidance for the reader, a closer connection with the spoken word and an understanding of grammatical structures (Parkes, 1992 [2016]: 37).

With the revolutionary introduction of the moveable type in England by William Caxton (d. 1492) at the end of the fifteenth century, a standard system of punctuation was urgently required. These pressures gradually favoured the use of *positurae*, not only thanks to their simplicity and their suitability for smaller scripts, but also because they emerged from the manuscript tradition on which early printing was heavily based (Parkes, 1992 [2016]: 50). Their use, however, was gradual and regulated by the needs of printers: from as early as the end of the fifteenth century, punctuation began to act as a remedy to problems existing in printing workshops, caused by the lack of funding and scarcity of primary sources (see Howard-Hill, 2006; further details available in Chapter 7, section 7.2).

During most of the sixteenth and the seventeenth centuries, punctuation was used both for prosodic and syntactic reasons, with some new inventions arising as evolved forms of *positurae*. In Italy, Aldus Manutius (1449–1515), an ambitious Venetian printer of classical texts, popularised the typographic practice of ending sentences with the colon and the period. He also made occasional use of parentheses, created the modern comma by lowering the virgule, and invented the semicolon (Parkes, 1992 [2016]: 49). The semicolon in particular was a child of experimentation, which came after a time when manuscripts had been filled with impressively creative ways of indicating the finest prosodic and syntactic nuances.[7] While some punctuation marks had a short life (for example, the pilcrow,[8] used to signpost passages of particular interest; see Houston, 2013: 3–24), the semicolon was not just lucky enough to survive a long time; it was useful from both a prosodic and a syntactic point of view. Easy to remember, it was a blend between the colon and the period, and struck a welcome balance between too short and too long a pause (see Parkes, 1992 [2016]: 49).

By the end of the seventeenth century, the exclamation and the question marks had officially joined the growing family of English punctuation. The presumed history of these two marks is one that tells how punctuation also stemmed from everyday words, and not just *positurae.* The exclamation mark is said to have sourced from *iō*, a Latin word expressing 'joy' (comparable to English *hurrah*), which was later shortened in writing to an *o* with a superscript *I* (see Brown, 2019: 84; Hazrat, 2022: 25, 112). Likewise, the question mark seems to be a descendant of the Latin abbreviation *Qo*, which stood for the word *quæstio.* The two letters were sometimes written on top of each other and formed an archaic version of <?> (Spector, 2017: 234; Brown, 2019: 84). By the time the exclamation and the questions marks arose, the *punctus elevatus* had officially given way to the comma, the colon and the dash (Brown, 2024). As argued by Parkes (1992 [2016]: 40), the growth in the number of different punctuation marks allowed for improvements in the ways in which various marks were used, so that texts provided clearer grammatical structures and conveyed more precise semantic nuances.

While printed books underwent a process of format standardisation between the sixteenth and the seventeenth centuries, during the same period punctuation marks in handwritten manuscripts were subjected to a whole different fate. In handwriting, the inventory and frequency of punctuation was heavily idiosyncratic. Salmon (1999: 43) mentions a manuscript authored by Shakespeare, and in particular a section of the play *Sir Thomas More* (McKnight, 1968 [1928]: 192), as an illustrative example. Here, the illustrious playwright seems to have used commas very abundantly, to the exclusion of all other punctuation marks. Perhaps in hope of regulating some of these idiosyncrasies in the use of English punctuation, the scholarship of the time focused

[7] The semicolon was not present among the punctuation units described by John Hart, the most prominent commentator on punctuation among the early English grammarians. Hart is also a pioneer in describing the comma, the colon and the period both from a syntactic and from a rhetorical point of view (Salmon, 1999: 22). More information about Hart is available in Chapter 6, section 6.2.

[8] The pilcrow, derived from the capitulum mark, is however still used occasionally, for example in some Bible editions.

its efforts increasingly on identifying principles for a more predictable use of punctuation both in handwriting and in print. In particular, two different schools of thought were formed. For the elocutionists, who looked back at the scribal tradition, punctuation was exclusively a way of indicating pauses and a guide for reading aloud. According to the grammarians, who were a group of linguistic innovators, punctuation was a way to support the new tendency of reading silently, a predictable marking system to show grammatical structure (Parkes, 1992 [2016]: 89–92; Brown, 2019: 83).

Although this debate became more fierce in the eighteenth century, the seeds had already been planted in the sixteenth and the seventeenth centuries: among the earliest theoreticians, George Puttenham (1529–1590) and Simon Daines (mid-seventeenth century) had tried to establish a hierarchy of punctuation marks on the basis of their pause values, which means that punctuation was, for them, a prosodic instrument (Brown, 2019: 83; 2024). Ben Jonson (1572–1637), instead, had indicated punctuation as a useful tool for segmenting text into syntactic units, thus spearheading what would become a widespread trend from the second half of the seventeenth century (Brown, 2019: 83; 2024). A more sustained dissemination of syntactic punctuation rules was made possible, in the nineteenth century, by the Industrial Revolution, which encouraged mass-scale production of paper and typesetting tools. The use of new technology, however, meant that new restrictions were suddenly imposed on spelling and punctuation. The invention of electrical telegraphy, which used a small number of transmission codes, and typewriters, based on a restricted range of keys, are probably the most relevant examples. With the telegraph, dots and dashes were the only instruments used to establish a binary communication system using electromechanical induction (Nellist, 1992: 83). Likewise, the first prototype of the typewriter, patented in 1867, only contained a small number of punctuation marks, namely ; $ - . , ? / . (Houston, 2013: 94–95).

If on one hand some technology encouraged simplification in the breadth of punctuation available, the nineteenth century was also, on the other hand, a time of excessive uses of the same few punctuation marks. During this time, written English went through a period of linguistic 'anxiety', resulting in excessively complex and long sentences, which required substantial help from punctuation. In order to offset the escalating complexities of English syntax, Henry Watson Fowler (1858–1933) and Francis George Fowler (1871–1918) published a book called *The King's English* (1906), the first of many from then on to argue for a lighter use of punctuation (Brown, 2019: 84; 2024). The need for simplification arose from public complaint; by this time, punctuation was far from being a concern of just a handful of well-educated elite individuals. By the early twentieth century, elementary schools were obliged to provide free schooling and to meet certified standards of education, all of which boosted average education levels (Mitch, 1992: 2). Reading became an activity that many people took delight in, and it is likely that many had strong opinions about how virtuously or how despicably pointed were various books of their time.

The gradual shift towards modernity was sealed by the turn of the twentieth century, which saw experimentation with punctuation largely for creative, expressive purposes. Some common examples are those of propaganda statements during the totalitarian era in Europe, which would not shy away from reporting quotes from those involved in the Second World War in order to spread hope (e.g. "I trust I may live to see Hitlerism destroyed" were Chamberlain's final words, quoted in the *Nottingham Evening Post* on 3 September 1939). The prolific use of some punctuation marks was the natural outgrowth of a prolonged sense of insecurity that had made its way among newspress businesses from the early twentieth century onwards, due to what may have been perceived as a crushing competition coming from the invention of the radio and television (see Hayes, 1999). The use of the exclamation mark in "Men Walk on Moon!" in the *Milwaukee Sentinel* (1969) could be interpreted, perhaps provokingly, as an attempt to take everyone's attention away from the black-and-white television images of two men hopping over the moon's surface, and turn it back to the newspapers.

By the early twentieth century, punctuation became the socially and linguistically expected norm. Proof of how deeply entwined punctuation was with written communication was the fact that the intentional omission of it became one of the many eccentric communicative tools in the hands of the modernist writers. Examples include those of James Joyce (1882–1941) and Virginia Woolf (1882–1941), who used the absence of punctuation marks in their texts to indicate thought-immersive psychological states (see Joyce, 1916, 1922; Woolf, 1925, 1927). The later part of the twentieth century saw various creative sparks in the uses of punctuation marks: in the 1960s, for example, advertising agent Martin Speckter (1915–1988) invented the *interrobang* (‽). Speckter's obituary in *The New York Times* from 16 February 1988 provides some context on the circumstances that led the man, a retired advertising executive, editor of *TYPEtalks* magazine and typography enthusiast, to create the interrobang. Much like Aldus Manutius, Speckter was driven by a practical need to find originality in his advertising endeavours, and pursued innovation doing what his Renaissance colleague had done centuries earlier with the semicolon: marrying up two already existing punctuation marks. Thus, the exclamation and the question marks were combined to form what was intended as the written alternative to a dismissive shrug. It was perhaps the lack of a syntactic purpose that eventually led the interrobang to extinction (see Houston, 2013: 29–44).

Discussion Material

1. Is it possible to add to the definitions of punctuation provided in section 5.1 by identifying phonetic vs. non-phonetic punctuation marks? Justify your answer.
2. Provide example sentences where the general graphematic functions for each punctuation mark provided in section 5.1 are not followed as closely, or not at all.
3. Identify examples of line-final word division in the present chapter. Discuss the principles used to split words across lines in your selected examples.
4. How is punctuation in novels different from that used elsewhere, for example on internet blogs or your favourite social media? Provide contextual examples.
5. Which punctuation marks do you use more and less frequently, and why? Compare your answers with those of others in class.

Recommendations for Reading

Brown, Adam (2019), *Understanding and Teaching English Spelling: A Strategic Guide*, New York: Routledge, pp. 81–89.

Jajdelska, Elspeth (2007), *Silent Reading and the Birth of the Narrator*, Toronto: University of Toronto Press.

Kirchhoff, Frank and Beatrice Primus (2016), 'Punctuation', in Vivian Cook and Des Ryan (eds), *The Routledge Handbook of the English Writing System*, London and New York: Routledge, pp. 93–109.

Meletis, Dimitrios and Christa Dürscheid (2022), *Writing Systems and their Use: An Overview of Grapholinguistics*, Berlin and Boston: De Gruyter Mouton, pp. 141–147.

Parkes, Malcolm B. (1992), *Pause and Effect: An Introduction to the History of Punctuation in the West*, Aldershot: Ashgate [reprinted in 2016 by Routledge], pp. 1–61.

6 Capitalisation

6.1 Defining capitalisation

The previous chapter focused on punctuation. The discussion addressed the question of whether punctuation marks can be considered to be graphemes, and which graphic forms belong to the punctuation inventory. The chapter also gave a brief history of English punctuation, with a view to explaining that the overarching syntactic function of English punctuation has come about over a long, laboured process of development. This chapter addresses capitalisation in ways that are similar to those followed in the previous chapter, posing the question of how this category of graphic units in the English writing system is understood from a graphematic point of view. Capitalisation in English results, in printing, from the alternation between *uppercase* and *lowercase* letters in the Roman alphabet (e.g. <A> vs. <a>, <B> vs. <b>, <C> vs. <c>, and so on), and, in handwriting, between *majuscule* and *minuscule* forms of the same letters (see Coulmas, 1996a: 532; Cook, 2004: 110–112; see also Chapter 4, section 4.1 and this chapter, section 6.2).

As mentioned in Chapter 5 (section 5.1), capitalisation is sometimes considered, by those who have a more permissive theoretical understanding of punctuation (e.g. by Nunberg et al., 2002, also referenced in Hartmann and Szczepaniak, 2023: 70), to belong to punctuation, due to some of the linguistic functions that capitalisation shares with it. Hartmann and Szczepaniak (2023: 70) argue that said linguistic functions are primarily two: that of marking the beginning of a sentence (a function complementary to that of the full stop) and that of drawing attention to specific words within a sentence (a function analogical to that of the single and double quotation marks). These two functions are further elaborated on in the following two bullet points:

- The task of marking the beginning of a sentence is fulfilled when capitalisation occurs in *sentence-initial position*. This process enables syntactic parsing and involves capitalising the first letter of the first word, which therefore is uppercase, in contrast to all the other lowercase letters. While this type of capitalisation occurs relatively predictably in printed English, there are exceptions usually dependent on format and style. One of these exceptions is that of the use of SMALL CAPS, where all of the letters required to form a word spelling are uppercase. Another exception is that of Title Case, a style frequently used when creating bibliographic entries, consisting of the uppercasing of each individual word in a sentence. In bibliographic entries that follow this format (as exemplified in the bibliography contained in this textbook), nouns, adjectives and verbs are uppercase for book titles (but not for chapter and research article titles), regardless of their sentence position.

- The task of drawing attention to specific words within a sentence is fulfilled by exceptionally using capitalisation in *sentence-internal positions*. This is a communicative function comparable to that of vertical punctuation marks (see Chapter 5, section 5.1), where the writer comes out of his or her usual covert position to point to a specific word or groups of words. Some examples are provided below, building upon the material available in Brown (2019: 99–100):[1]
  - The pronoun *I*, which may have arisen by analogy with old-fashioned tense markers in English and, perhaps, also due to the fact that pen strokes were naturally elongated in more casual, spontaneous handwriting.
  - Reverential appellative nouns, such as *King Charles III*, but not when the words *king* and *queen* are used as common nouns, and only occasionally in *sir* or *madam*.
  - Names of individuals or locations, for instance *Peter*, *London*, *America*, *Mount Etna* and *the Great Pyramid of Giza*.
  - Geographically derived attributes, for example in *a European* (noun), *my Indian friend* (adjective).
  - Other geographical details, for example in *I'm from the North*. This pattern generally does not apply to cardinal directions, so for example in *Sheffield is north of London*.
  - Elements in the universe, e.g. *Mars*, *the Milky Way* and *the Earth*.
  - Religious attributes, for instance in *a Protestant Bible*, and *a Catholic writer*.

[1] See also Wikipedia's entries on capitalisation (<en.wikipedia.org/wiki/Capitalization>, <en.wikipedia.org/wiki/Capitalization_in_English> [accessed Jan. 2025]), which provide a more democratic view of capitalisation uses in English and have inspired, with due caution, some of the examples provided here.

- Deities and personifications, e.g. *God, Fate, Destiny.*
- Chronological indications, e.g. *Tuesday, March,* while seasons such as *spring* are not capitalised consistently.
- Labels and logos, for example *Nike, Audi, Sprite,* with exceptions when brand names become more widely used as common nouns, e.g. *the hoover.*
- All other proper nouns not mentioned explicitly in the list provided above. Examples in which capitalised proper nouns are likely to be required are official documents, where individuals are sometimes asked to spell out their full name and then sign below either electronically or by pen.

The crucial question underlying the analogy made so far with punctuation is whether capitalised units, and their corresponding lowercase and minuscule versions, can be taken to be individual graphemes, as with punctuation, or whether they should be understood as allographs of each other (according to the definition of the allograph provided in Chapter 4, section 4.3) (Meletis and Dürscheid, 2022: 158). Unfortunately, capitalisation is one of the most neglected areas of discussion in grapholinguitics to date, so providing a precise solution to the problem posed above is not as straightforward as it may have been for punctuation. There are, however, some brief references to the grapholinguistic understanding of capitalisation made so far in the literature that consider both sides of the matter (graphemes vs. allographs) and lead us towards a potential answer.

According to Sampson (1985: 16; see also Meletis and Dürscheid, 2022: 158), in particular, patterns such as those outlined in the bullet points above are sufficiently predictable to be able to consider uppercase and lowercase variants[2] of a letter of the alphabet as individual graphemes. In addition to being predictable, the patterns exemplified above are also linguistically meaningful. Just as for punctuation, the use of capitalisation, often in combination with punctuation marks like the full stop, can provide a neat syntactic, morphological and semantic separation between two different interpretations of two adjacent sentences. The issue is immediately apparent when capitalisation and punctuation split off propositional verbs, which usually gain a different meaning from the original meaning that a verb has on its own. Compare,

[2] In the remaining part of section 6.1 especially, 'uppercase' and 'lowercase' are used as less clunky, more efficient synonyms of 'capitalised' and 'non-capitalised', thus also implicitly indicating majuscule and minuscule letters.

for example, *Jack finally passes. For a scientist, it is not a surprise.* vs. *Jack finally passes for a scientist. It is not a surprise …*[3]

Capitalisation on its own can also be the basis for lexical 'minimal pairs' (compare punctuation in Chapter 5, section 5.1), sometimes accompanied by a change in meaning and pronunciation. Examples of this kind include the word *job* (work, usually in the context of employement), pronounced /dʒɒb/, and *Job* (the biblical character), pronounced /dʒəʊb/. Context sentences where these two forms would appear are, respectively, as follows: *I finally managed to get a job, after applying to no less than ten different positions* vs. *The Book of Job is an underappreciated segment of the Bible.*[4] Moreover, capitalisation can help to disambiguate a semantic value from another within the same spelling form and pronunciation. Examples include the following: *Turkey* (the country) vs. *turkey* (the animal), *Catholic* (of Catholic faith) vs. *catholic* (widely embracing), *China* (the country) vs. *china* (porcelain), *Conservative* (member of the Conservative Party) vs. *conservative* (someone opposed to change and innovation), and *May* (the month) vs. *may* (to be possible) (additional examples available in Brown, 2019: 101; see also the *titanic/Titanic* example mentioned in Chapter 2, section 2.2).[5] Examples like those given above can also help one to distinguish between a generalised indication of an object and a specific instance of that object, so that, within the category of elements in the universe described above, there is a difference between *a moon*, intended as any natural satellite which could be found orbiting a planet, and *the Moon*, intended as the Earth's only natural satellite.

With that said, the situation involving capitalisation is more complicated than what it may seem from the examples discussed so far, as the understanding of uppercase and lowercase letters as individual graphemes is challenged by the way in which capitalisation operates in English. Capitalisation is not always as substantially contrastive as default graphemes may be; in other words, a large number of examples of capitalisation do not change in meaning following developments on a syntactic or morphological level. One of the most widely known processes involving capitalisation is that of lexicalisation through the formation of *acronyms*,[6]

[3] Compare examples on Wikipedia, <https://en.wikipedia.org/wiki/English_phrasal_verbs> [accessed September 2025]).

[4] Compare examples on Wikipedia, <https://en.wikipedia.org/wiki/Capitonym> [accessed September 2025]).

[5] Examples available on Wikipedia (<https://en.wikipedia.org/wiki/Capitonym> [accessed September 2025]).

[6] In the lexicalisation process, acronyms are intended as "instances of recruitment of linguistic material to enrich the lexicon" (Hopper and Traugott, 1993: 127).

which are short forms of earlier multi-word phrases or sentences pronounced as individual words (Brown, 2019: 102). These short forms usually retain the same meaning as the original multi-word forms from which they derive and help writers to get across their intended meaning in a more succinct way. The making of acronyms in English is a relatively simple linguistic process involving, in Brown's opinion (2019: 102–103), five distinguishable steps, which are summarised in the next few paragraphs below. The common thread across these five steps is the idea that, by virtue of the fact that uppercase and lowercase letters can be interchanged without causing variation in meaning (and are therefore non-contrastive) from the original unit, shorter versions of an earlier multi-word form are created.

The first stage in the formation of an acronym consists in the creation, whether spontaneous or not, of an *initialism*, namely acronyms which are not pronounced as words. Initialisms are formed by capitalising the first letter of the words that one wants to abbreviate, followed by a full stop placed immediately after each first capitalised letter (Brown, 2019: 102). For example, 'United States of America' would become *U.S.A.* and 'United Kingdom' would become *U.K.*[7] The second step of the process involves eliminating the full stops, which gradually become redundant once the meaning of the initials is established and reasonably widespread. Thus, it is not uncommon to find, for the respective examples mentioned above, forms like *USA* and *UK* (examples from Brown, 2019: 102).[8] While omitting full stops from capitalised initials at this stage usually leads to no problems with interpreting the meaning of the abbreviated words, it is also possible to experience some confusion when reading fully capitalised lines, for example in USA TO MAKE A DEAL WITH CHINA USING IT COMMUNICATION. The most obscure unit in this example is IT, which stands for 'Information Technology',

[7] This first step may also occur with words being abbreviated using more than just one letter, for example in *Mister Michael Jackson*, which would become *Mr. M. Jackson* or *Mr M. Jackson* (Brown, 2019: 102).

[8] However, there are some differences in the ways in which full stops are used in relevant examples between American and British English. While, in American English, acronyms often do not use full stops (e.g. FBI, NASA, USA), acronyms in British English tend to use full stops more frequently (e.g. P.M. and A.M. may sometimes still be used). More recently, however, British English has shown greater tendency to follow the American English model, dropping the full stops from across several acronyms (e.g. B.B.C. > BBC, E.U. > EU and V.I.P. > VIP). Some scholars and readers might rightly beg to disagree, arguing that American English uses full stops more frequently (see Brown, 2019: 102 for opposing views). Confusion on the matter is the result of a fast-changing landscape.

but may be confused with the pronoun 'it' (an additional example along these lines is available in Brown, 2019: 102).

The third step in the making of acronyms involves pronunciation and signals the stage where the initials are not pronounced anymore as a set of full words but as an actual abbreviation, due to the fact that the meaning has by now become almost universally acknowledged. This step normally affects longer strings of initials, so for example *UNICEF* is pronounced as a word rather than as a string of initials (example from Brown, 2019: 102–103), while the word *B&B* can be pronounced both as initials and in its full form, 'Bed and Breakfast'. It should be made clear, at this point, that only words that reach this third step of development can formally be understood as acronyms, and not all forms reach all of the steps outlined here, for various linguistic or extra-linguistic reasons. At this point, the term *acronym* is officially used to indicate words that are abbreviated using initials and that usually end up being pronounced as a whole word (Brown, 2019: 102).

Abbreviations of this type normally contain vowels as part of the constituent initials, so that the spelling form can be pronounced as a word relatively straightforwardly. Those that do not have vocalic elements in their new spelling are subject to ambiguities of the type illustrated for *B&B* above. Other, similar examples are that of the form *ATM*, which stands for 'automated teller machine' and *JPEG*, which stands for 'Joint Photographic Experts Group' (for a slightly different argument, see Brown, 2019: 102).[9] When creating easily pronounceable acronyms is not immediately possible just from using the first letter of each word in a string of words, abbreviations may be formed by taking the first syllable of each word in order to make a new spelling form. These examples are known in linguistics as *syllabic acronyms*. An example of this category of acronyms is that of the word *Interpol*, which stems from a blend of 'international' and 'police' (further information on syllabic acronyms is available in Jackson, 2002: 14; Brown, 2019: 103).

The fourth step in the creation of an acronym consists in turning the abbreviated word into lowercase letters, with the exception of the first letter, which remains capitalised (e.g. the form *Nasa*, which comes from 'National Aeronautics and Space Administration'). The fifth stage, instead, consists in taking away the first capitalised letter and replacing it with a lowercase letter, so that the abbreviated word becomes unrecognisable in its true essence of an acronym (Brown, 2019: 103).

[9] The abbreviation *BBQ* is also a noteworthy example, as it is usually not pronounced as a series of letters by native speakers of English, but it is in other countries where English is not spoken as a first language (e.g. Italy).

It is not rare, for example, to see the form *asap* entirely lowercased. Other examples include *taser*, which comes from 'Thomas A. Swift's Electric Rifle', and *laser*, which comes from 'Light Amplification by the Stimulated Emission of Radiation' (additional examples available in Brown, 2019: 103).

As we have seen with the examples described so far, the interchangeable qualities of uppercase and lowercase letters are paramount in the making of initialisms and acronyms. Short forms available as the product of the fifth stage of development illustrated above feature lowercase versions of what were previously capitalised word-initial letters of a longer string of words. In view of these examples, therefore, it would seem appropriate to suggest that the alternation between uppercase and lowercase letters is one that resembles that of *free allography* (i.e. non-contrastive variation occurring irrespectively of the position of the uppercase and lowercase letters, see Meletis and Dürscheid, 2022: 155, 158) rather than default graphemes. In this respect, some parallels may be identified with punctuation, for example, as the same individual punctuation marks are likely to be found in different syntactic positions. In other words, capitalisation, like punctuation, has default rules for each individual graphic unit within its inventory regardless of where in a text a given sentence structure is found.

The analogy given above, however, is not entertained in recent grapholinguistic work as sufficient for free allography. According to Meletis and Dürscheid (2022: 158), for example, capitalisation behaves in a way that is uniquely context dependent and therefore cannot be equated to the behaviour of punctuation. Uppercase and lowercase letters, the authors argue, "are not separate graphemes but syntagmatic graphematic allographs" (Meletis and Dürscheid, 2022: 158), namely allographs conditioned by their linguistic contexts. Capitalisation is often *pragmatically* conditioned, thus making it heavily dependent on ad-hoc morphological and semantic scenarios. Pragmatic contexts can be highly specific and determined by idiosyncrasies, in ways that make the idea of free allographic variation difficult to demonstrate. There are several examples that show why capitalisation may be an instance of syntagmatic allography instead of an example of free allography.

A compelling example given by Brown (2019: 100) of the ad-hoc nature of capitalisation as an allographic event is that of the logo *Adidas*, which is actually always lowercased, as in *adidas*, despite it being a proper name. Likewise, there are examples of public figures who normally spell their name with lowercase letters, including American professor *john a. powell* and British musician *dodie.* Today's English is also seeing an increasing number of examples of words where capital letters are found in the middle of a word, originally formed by blending two individual word items. This phenomenon is known as *bicapitalisation* and includes, for example, words like *ExxonMobil*. Another compelling example is that of the word *PowerPoint*, which is used in an educational context (example from Brown, 2019: 100). The main reason why these words defy regular capitalisation conventions is that of a strategic marketing choice (Brown, 2019: 101), and it is interesting to note how widespread some of these words are becoming in everyday vocabulary.

Other examples show that capitalisation in English may be pragmatically conditioned not only by the writer's idiosyncratic choices, but also by the purposes for which a word is written. These include the capitalisation of epithets or designations, for instance in *mayor*, *chancellor*, or even *reverend* and *priest*. Confusion over whether these items should be capitalised or not usually arises from conflicting, irregular examples in the English language, where forms like *President Roosevelt* are capitalised but others like *Roosevelt was president of the United States of America* are not (see Brown, 2019: 101). A similar example of pragmatically conditioned variation in sentences denoting roles and positions is that of *Frank Smith is the deputy director* vs. *Deputy Director Frank Smith*. Interestingly, the variation arising from the inverted syntactic arrangement shown here does not always apply to all workers within a business company and across different business companies (see Brown, 2019: 101), which further highlights the ad-hoc nature of capitalisation.

6.2 Development of capitalisation

As the examples discussed so far have shown, capitalisation can be a complex linguistic transaction between the writer and the reader. The frequency of occurrence of this linguistic transaction in written English today is always implicitly regulated by our cognitive needs, and an appropriate share of uppercase and lowercase letters in the right proportions in a text is key for one to read efficiently. The crucial consideration when using capitalisation is that the reader is not confronted with an excessive number of capitalised words on a single syntactic segment, As With This Example Provided Here (compare the example in Crystal, 2015: ix–x). A large number of capital letters can make writing look cluttered and quirky, though this was not always the case in the past. The linguistic functions of capitalisation that we use today, and its ambiguous contrastive vs. non-contrastive graphematic purposes, have arisen from a complex process of diachronic development that saw capitalisation going through different widespread conventions, from stylistic to functional ones.

Initially, capitalisation served as a purely stylistic feature, originating from the use of different scripts in written Latin. In the Roman Empire (including Roman-invaded Britain from 43 AD), different writing scripts were part of the visual apparatus that characterised the media on which writing appeared. In particular, capital letters were the default letterforms used when etching in stone, since they took less effort than any other shape when carving lines using a chisel and a hammer. Capital letters usually took up a pre-determined square-box space and appeared adjacently to each other, leaving no room for blank spaces and other punctuation marks of any kinds (Sampson, 1985: 110–111). Lowercase letters, on the other hand, derive from a writing style used in Roman handwriting known as *cursive*. It was a more rounded writing style that started out as a series of letters formed individually and ended up becoming a string of rapidly written letters made with few (or even single) pen strokes (Sampson, 1985: 111). Within the category of cursive writing, Sampson (1985: 111) argues, "a 'minuscule' hand developed in which letters differed in height".

With the decline and fall of the Roman Empire, between the fourth and the sixth centuries AD, the Roman standard gave way to stylistic conventions arising from 'national hands', including Italian semi-cursive minuscule and the Carolingian style (Sampson, 1985: 111). The Carolingian style in particular afforded scribes the ability to devise text organisation and presentation afresh (Saenger, 1997: 106–107; see Chapter 5, section 5.2). A typical attribute of early manuscripts from which the Carolingian style tried to distance itself, for example, is that of *diminuendo*. This feature affects the first line of a new text or chapter and consists of the use of a large-sized capital letter, usually followed immediately by a smaller letter, then an even smaller one, and so on, gradually reaching a lowercase letter size used by default for the majority of the text (Parkes, 1992 [2016]: 25, 34, 175).

While avoiding *diminuendo*, Carolingian scribes followed the Irish and English traditions of using decorated *litterae notabiliores* ('more notable letters'). These were first letters of new text sections laid out to the left of the first line and made to appear in a much larger size than the rest of the letters in the same line (Parkes, 1992 [2016]: 1). Line-initial 'notable' capitalisation occurred in many manuscripts of the Frankish kingdom written in Carolingian style (see, for example, those mentioned by Parkes, 1992 [2016]: 31, 33). The earliest example of texts copied using *litterae notabiliores* is the Bible of Maudramnus (Amiens, Bibliothèque municipale, MSS 6, 7, 9, 11, 12), called as such after Maudramnus, an abbot who lived in Corbie at the end of the eighth century (Saenger, 1997: 107). This text, written in Latin, features the use of capitalisation not only in the first letter of the line, but across all letters of the first line of a new book within the Bible, albeit these being capitalised in less prominent sizes than the *littera notabilior*.

As mentioned briefly in Chapter 5 (section 5.2), the Carolingian style gradually made extensive use of blank spaces between individual letters, but these were not always present during the Middle Ages across all texts from both Insular and Continental Europe. Instead, other strategies for legibility were sometimes put in place. Of particular interest in this sense is the reference made by Saenger (1997: 59) to the fact that, between the ninth and the twelfth centuries, capital letters were sometimes used both word-initially and word-finally in order to demarcate individual words in texts where blank spaces were absent or sparsely used. Psycholinguistic research, Saenger (1997: 59) continues, has shown that word boundaries are important for word identification during the reading process, as they feed peripheral vision with the necessary elements for recognising words immediately when reading quickly (see also Chapter 8, section 8.1).

The practice of demarcating individual words using capital letters on both ends of each word was reserved especially to proper nouns, which were considered to be the most important units from a semantic perspective. Among the capitalised letters used more frequently word-finally in nouns, <R>, <S> and <A> were most popular in medieval manuscripts, with <S> being markedly more recurrent among the three (e.g. in words like *AgnuS* 'lamb' from Berangar of Tour's *Rescripta contra Lanfrancum*, Herzog August Bibliothek, Weissenburg 101: 211, as cited in Saenger, 1997: 61). The practice of capitalising proper nouns went through periods of flourishing and decline by the late Middle Ages, but was temporarily brought back by Renaissance scribes, who in turn inspired new typesetting rules from the late fifteenth century, whereby only the first letter of a word was capitalised (Saenger, 1997: 62). In the average sixteenth- and seventeenth-century printing workshop, material letters were stored in boxes, known as 'cases', and typesetters grabbed individual letters from these boxes every time they needed more material for composition. Usually, capitalised letters were stored in the upper case (hence 'uppercase', as opposed to 'majuscule' > Latin *maius* 'greater') and non-capitalised letters were stored in a case just underneath the capitals (hence 'lowercase', as opposed to minuscule > Latin *minus* 'smaller') (see also Mosley, 2009: 174; Parkes, 1992 [2016]: 302).

Capitalisation in printed books was varied and inconsistent, especially during the sixteenth century, despite the fact that different grammarians shared relatively similar opinions on the matter. John Hart, in his first book on English orthography (1551 [1955]), written with the goal of providing guidelines on how to use English spelling and punctuation, writes that capital letters should be present at the onset of each sentence, especially after the "full point" (the period), the "wonderer" (the exclamation mark) and the "asker" (the question mark), as well as for the "proper name of everi thing" and semantically important common nouns (Hart, 1551 [1955]: 155; Salmon, 1999: 22). Among the seventeenth-century English grammarians, Butler (1633: 4) mentions that, unlike "vulgar" (i.e. lowercase) letters, capital letters had to mark "appellatives", which, as nouns, are key elements in written language (for example, 'Book', 'Noun' and 'Script'). A little later, Wharton (1654: 22) adds that capital letters should be used to mark new "verses" and the personal pronoun *I* (Salmon, 1999: 38).

After the English Restoration of 1660, common nouns became capitalised increasingly more frequently. According to Crystal (2019: 69), examples of capitalised words included "titles (*Sir*, *Lady*), forms of address (*Father*, *Mistris*) and personified nouns". Capitalisation, Crystal continues, would also be used for emphatic purposes both on words and entire sentences. By the eighteenth century, sentence-internal capitalisation began to take a more prominent place in the historical development of English, perhaps triggered by printers' need to achieve a systematic pattern for using capitalisation correctly, as well as a desire to attain aesthetically pleasing results (Crystal, 2019: 69). By the late eighteenth century, however, grammarians began to complain about the excessive use of capitalisation in English, pointing out that it caused untidiness in writing. In 1861, for instance, grammarian Simon Kerl states that "capital letters should not be used without good reason, or when small letters would express the sense as well or better" (Kerl, 1861: 97). Comments like those made by Kerl caused a decrease in the average number of capitalised nouns in written English, allowing rules to align more closely with those of our present day (Crystal, 2019: 69).

In the meantime, the gradual disappearance of sentence-internal capitalisation in English was heavily criticised by American statesman Benjamin Franklin (1706–1790). He claimed in a letter written to Noah Webster (1758–1843) that, in the past,

> [...] all substantives were begun with a capital, in which we imitated our mother tongue, the German. This was more particularly useful to those who were not well acquainted with the English, there being such a prodigious number of our words that are both verbs and substantives, and spelt in the same manner, though often accented differently in pronunciation. This method has, by the fancy of printers, of late years been entirely laid aside; from an idea, that suppressing the capitals shews the character

> to greater advantage; those letters, prominent above the line, disturbing its even, regular appearance. (Franklin, 1789: 84, as cited in Crystal, 2019: 69)

The American nation's desire to hold on to sentence-internal capitalisation was made obvious in the example of the US Constitution of 1787, whose first lines read as follows:

> We the People of the United States, in Order to form a more perfect Union, establish Justice, insure domestic Tranquility, provide for the common defence, promote the general Welfare, and secure the Blessings of Liberty to ourselves and our Posterity, do ordain and establish this Constitution for the United States of America.[10]

An unrelated, but still relevant, example of the thread connecting American English with capitalisation is that of the long-held tradition of the US Navy of writing communication using uppercase letters. This tradition first began when the US Navy, in the nineteenth century, introduced teletype machine communication as a protocol for standard internal communication. In 2013, however, new changes were introduced by US Fleet Cyber Command manager James McCarty as a result of dissatisfaction among the younger soldiers, who felt that they were being shouted at every time they received an official communication from the US Navy (BBC News, 2013; see also Horobin, 2021). This example shows the extent to which the text messaging culture of the last few decades has influenced recent linguistic developments, initiating a new era of instability in the uses of capitalisation.

The relationship between capitalisation and technology over the last three decades has been a turbulent one, as it has been characterised by ambiguities which have created a sharp contrast between frowned-upon idiosyncrasies and the rise of new 'standards'. With the advent of SMS technology, which became more widespread from the 1990s, capitalisation began to be used following non-traditional rules, which nonetheless became widespread on a large scale (see especially Crystal, 2008). Examples of capitalised words that have become standard in text language since the introduction of the first text messaging devices include initialisms like *OMG* for 'oh my god', *LOL* for 'laugh(ing) out loud', *BRB* for 'be right back' and *IMO* for 'in my opinion' – all of which will be undoubtedly familiar to most readers. There are technologically induced reasons behind the widespread use of these relatively new

[10] Also cited on Wikipedia's entry for English capitalisation (<en.wikipedia.org/wiki/Capitalization_in_English> [accessed January 2025]).

conventions. SMS-based communication, in its early days, involved the use of abbreviations, in order to comply with the character limit of 160 characters for each individual SMS. During the first decades of text messaging technology, each individual SMS had to be paid for independently, and there were few, if any, service-provider contract offers with unlimited text messages included. Nowadays, at least at the time of writing this book, most modern devices allow for message concatenation, and monthly phone plans are so popular that the majority of people can send virtually unlimited messages of unlimited length to any addressee.

While technology has changed, the principle behind abbreviation remains the same: abbreviating words is efficient, as it enables users to convey information in a less energy- and time-demanding way than spelling out full words. Some features of text language have become so widespread (e.g. *BTW* for 'by the way' and *IDK* for 'I don't know') that they have found their way as acronyms into English vocabulary in everyone's phone autocorrect features, or have even spread outside of text language context and have gained popularity among speakers and internet users of younger generations (see also Cook, 2004: 193–204). Perhaps as a reaction to what is perceived as an unstoppable unruliness of internet-mediated communication, on 24 September every year the US celebrates National Punctuation Day, a proud festival aiming to encourage and foster awareness of the importance of punctuation and capitalisation among school students. While, as discussed in this chapter, there are conceptual differences between capitalisation and punctuation, both of these elements of the English writing system are still treated as a whole in educational initiatives like that of the National Punctuation Day (compare Chapter 8, section 8.2 for additional insights into educational prescriptivism).

The renewed interest in shepherding individuals through the use of capitalisation has also spread beyond education and has resulted, for example, in the creation of different conventions for capitalising text across different academic and trade publishers. Today, several style guides can be consulted and some of them appear to be more suited for specific contexts than others, though there is no consensus on the matter. A Wikipedia search for 'style guides'[11] (to be taken with caution) gives a range of different options grouped according to nationality ('international', 'Australia', 'Canada', 'European Union', 'New Zealand', 'United Kingdom', 'United States') and, within each

[11] Wikipedia (<https://en.wikipedia.org/wiki/MHRA_Style_Guide> [accessed September 2025]).

nationality, sector-related manuals that are normally followed. The *MHRA Style Guide*, for example, is cited as suitable for academic use, especially in the humanities, in the United Kingdom; *The Chicago Manual of Style*, on the other hand, is cited more frequently as a reference manual for humanities-related editorial style in the United States. *The BBC News Style Guide* and *The Daily Telegraph Style Guide* are given as manuals to follow for journalism in the United Kingdom, while, in the United States, *The Associated Press Stylebook* and *The New York Times Manual of Style and Usage* seem to be preferred.

Each style guide imposes very strict rules of capitalisation, both for the main text of a piece of writing and its bibliography, and there are often different preferences among individuals working in the same sector. For example, I prefer using Harvard Style, which requires writers to capitalise the first word of a title, and any subtitles, as well as proper nouns; a colleague of mine might prefer using the Modern Language Association Style, which requires capitalisation not only of the first and last words of a title and subtitle, but also of all major words in between (except conjunctions, articles and prepositions). Individual preferences may depend on the academic journals in which each of us respectively publishes our research, and their referencing style requirements, though it is often the case, in academia, that a variety of different academic journals are targeted by the same individual scholar for publication. Challenges stemming from applying all these different rules are some of the several reasons why some publishers hire professional copy-editors and proofreaders when working with an author's manuscript for publication.

If on the one hand there are measures in place to ensure that writers abide to the correct standards – whatever these may be according to the platform in question – there are, on the other hand, contemporary public figures who appear to be very fond of an abnormal use of capitalisation. In a Twitter (now X) post published in 2018, Donald Trump stated the following:

> Despite the Democrat inspired laws on Sanctuary Cities and the Border being so bad and one sided, I have instructed the Secretary of Homeland Security not to let these large Caravans of people into our Country. It is a disgrace. We are the only Country in the World so naive! WALL.

Another Tweet from the same year reads as follows: "After having written many best selling books, and somewhat priding myself on my ability to write, it should be noted that the Fake News constantly likes to pore over my tweets looking for a mistake", Trump claimed. "I capitalize certain words only for emphasis, not b/c they should be capitalized!"

(see Kirby, 2018). *The Washington Post* (Lenivonitz, 2018) provides an interesting insight into the Fake News phenomenon:

> The first 33 times [Trump] used it, the term appeared in all-caps or capitalized properly, either FAKE NEWS or fake news, except for one instance of Fake News on Jan 15, 2017. But then he started trying to make it real, a Platonic Form that exists in the world like Beauty and Truth. For a while, he alternated between fake news and Fake News, slowly skewing toward the latter, until finally it was nearly always Fake News.

Some may see in Trump's tweets only a personal preference for a boisterous writing style; others might see an intentional cry for attention and a stubborn desire to encourage a sense of unruliness and disregard for what is considered to be default linguistic practice. Although these examples cannot be considered as anything more than idiosyncratic uses of capitalisation, the choices made by notable individuals like Donald Trump provide fascinating insights into nuances that can be expressed through capitalisation alone, and the power of technology in shaping up its uses.

Discussion Material

1. Discuss any other examples where capitalisation may be found in English in addition to the cases provided in section 6.1.
2. Drawing on the five stages of acronym-making discussed in section 6.1, propose three examples of new acronyms on the basis of frequently recurring expressions in your everyday language.
3. To what extent is capitalisation important for your reading experience? Discuss in class.
4. Comparing the history of capitalisation (section 6.2) with that of punctuation in English (Chapter 5, section 5.2), which seems more complex and why?
5. Look up your most commonly-used words in one of your messaging apps on your phone. What are some of the most recurring abbreviations, if any, and what do they stand for?

Recommendations for Reading

Brown, Adam (2019), *Understanding and Teaching English Spelling: A Strategic Guide*, New York: Routledge, pp. 49–66, 98–104.

Cook, Vivian (2004), *The English Writing System*, London: Edward Arnold, pp. 110–112, 193–204.

Crystal, David (2008), *Txtng: The Gr8 Db8*, Oxford: Oxford University Press.
Meletis, Dimitrios and Christa Dürscheid (2022), *Writing Systems and their Use: An Overview of Grapholinguistics*, Berlin and Boston: De Gruyter Mouton, pp. 155–158.
Salmon, Vivian (1999), 'Orthography and punctuation', in Roger Lass (ed.), *The Cambridge History of the English Language*, vol. 3: *1476–1776*, Cambridge: Cambridge University Press, pp. 13–55.

Part III

Connections

7 Sociology and bibliography

7.1 Interdisciplinary insights

The second section of this textbook (Part II) provided definitions useful for the study of the English writing system. Chapter 4 discussed definitions for the graph, the glyph and the grapheme, while also examining complexities in the uses of 'orthography', 'spelling' and 'script'. Chapters 5 and 6 respectively provided descriptions of punctuation and capitalisation, focusing on their internal mechanisms and functions, making some comparisons on the basis of their respective roles in English syntax and semantics, and describing their complex historical developments. This third section (Part III), titled 'Connections', establishes links with areas that inform our understanding of the English writing system and yet fall beyond the remits of English linguistics in its strict sense. In this final part of the textbook, in particular, readers are encouraged to reflect about the English writing system in a variety of contexts, exploring the relationship between written English on one hand, and *sociology*, *bibliography*, the *psychology of reading* and *literacy studies*, on the other. The third and last chapter in this section draws some brief conclusions, reflecting about this textbook's contribution to the study of the English writing system, offering thoughts about its limitations and giving suggestions for future work aimed at integrating this textbook.

While no attempt is made at comprehensiveness in terms of topics and time spans covered when discussing interdisciplinary connections involving the English writing system, the areas covered in this final part of the textbook are among the most widely explored topics in applied linguistic approaches to the English writing system. The arrangement of topics and the way in which they are presented in this third part of the book follow a logical line of argumentation. The present chapter, for example, begins by focusing on how variables in English orthography, especially orthographic variation and standardisation, can give us information about sociolinguistic issues, and then moves on to discussing the importance of bibliographic contexts for studies in the English writing system. Since, as we have seen, the introduction of printing technology in England initiated and widely disseminated a standardised form of English orthography, in addition to reducing the amount of variation existing in the number of different spelling forms available for the same individual words, the correlation established in this chapter between sociolinguistics and the study of book materiality represents a logical thread. Another obvious link is that established between bibliography, at the end of Chapter 7, and the psychology of reading, at the beginning of Chapter 8. Both of these areas of academic enquiry establish correlations between the English writing system and the written text, albeit being concerned with different research questions. Connections of the kind established above form, in turn, a coherent continuation of the topics discussed in Part II, as variables in English orthography of the type explained above (orthographic variation and standardisation) can be expressed through various components of the English writing system, including the graph, the glyph, the grapheme, punctuation and capitalisation. Aspects of orthography, spelling and script are also relevant in the study of the psychology of reading and literacy studies. In particular, they are addressed when issues such as literacy, reading performance, and the correlation between the way in which a text is designed and how reading comprehension occurs, are explored empirically.

Let us begin our interdisciplinary excursus by defining sociology. To echo the words of Pierre Bourdieu (1930–2002), one of the foremost scholars of sociological research, defining sociology cannot be separated from some of the most important questions addressed in this field of enquiry, as outlined in the following quote (as available in Murji et al, 2021: 7):

> Like all scientists, the sociologist attempts to establish laws, to grasp regularities, recurrent ways of being and to define their principle. Why do people do the things they do? Why, for example, do teachers' children do better at school than working class children? By 'why', I mean, 'how is it that …'? How is it that it happens like that in society and not otherwise?

Writing plays an important role in attempting to address sociolinguistic questions, primarily for two reasons, which are identified by Coulmas (2013: 8) as follows. First of all, writing is an objective sensory experience, and human beings are naturally oriented towards seeing written evidence as convincing. Thus, writing gives human beings an objective parameter upon which not only to construct their own view of the world but also to analyse the experiences of others, departing, for example, from the sociolinguistic questions (i.e. the 'how-is-it-that' of human behaviour) laid out by Bourdieu.

Secondly, and perhaps most importantly, writing is a means through which people determine social status, since the ability to write (or to write proficiently) is not the same for everyone on our planet. If an individual writes elegantly, he or she is perceived as being well educated, and therefore more likely to have a position in society which gives him or her high status and power. Matters of social status and power represent an important starting point for addressing some of the questions posed in Pierre Bourdieu's quote. "In all societies", Coulmas argues (2013: 8), "writing is associated with authority, that is, with an *auctor* – whence 'author' – one who sets forth written statements and is empowered to enforce obedience." Even more to the point, what matters in society is not only the ability to write at all, but also the ability to write *correctly*, that is to say, the ability to use written language according to the perceived standard (for the prescriptive definition of orthography, see Chapter 4, section 4.1). This in turn means that an individual who uses written English in a non-traditional form, that is to say, following non-standard English orthography, may not enjoy as much social authority as someone who abides by the expectations set by our society about what is acceptable as correct (see Milroy and Milroy, 2002: 2).

Among the most recent contributions to the topic of correctness and its social implications, there are at least two titles that give valuable insights into the way in which English orthography plays a role in society, namely Sebba's *Spelling and Society* (2007) and Horobin's *Does Spelling Matter?* (2013). Sebba's book, briefly mentioned in Chapter 4, section 4.2, is a seminal work on the relationship between writing and sociological issues, and argues that orthography has an important role among many as a symbol of cultural, historical and social identity. "In English today", Sebba argues (2007: 7), "*vulcanising a tyre* is not exactly the same as *vulcanizing a tire*": they may express two slightly different processes of making or repairing tyres or two individual professional approaches to doing the same job across different geographical areas (for example, the UK and the US). Other examples given by Sebba, taken from graffiti (compare Chapter 4, section 4.2), show, for instance, how "[c]ertain typically Creole pronunciations, such as /tiŋ/ for *thing*, are represented in the spelling by deviating from the conventional Standard English spellings; thus, <tings>" (Sebba, 2007: 3).[1] These misspellings,

[1] Note that the graffiti was found "[i]n a busy street in the inner city of Manchester, England, in 1995" (Sebba, 2007: 3).

the author continues, may or may not come from native, professional users of what Sebba (2007: 4) calls "a British variety of English-lexicon Creole, similar to Jamaican Creole" as a way of signalling orthographic features that mark a distinction from Standard English (Sebba, 2007: 5). Even if the example is not from someone familiar with 'Creole' because of first-hand knowledge, the writer clearly chose to spell some words in a way that, it seems, echoes the pronunciation of the variety identified by Sebba.

In order for variation in written English to have some social meaning, Sebba continues (2007: 32), it must occur within the boundaries of what is perceived as orthographically possible. That is to say, in order for a spelling variation example to be widely understood, it has to strike a form that falls in between a rigidly fixed standard, where no deviation from the agreed norm occurs, and a completely permissive outcome, where any possible spelling can be used. Sebba (2007: 33) eloquently explains the matter with the following example:

> For example, in English there is no alternative sequence of letters which would recognisably represent the word *damp*. Changing the vowel will produce a different word or nonword, and no credible alternatives are available for the consonant sounds. No meaningful variation is possible [...] On the other hand, we could imagine a situation where spelling norms specify a set of sound-letter correspondences but allow a free choice where alternatives exist. In such a case, our 'stewdent,' or anyone else, would be free to write <thought>, <thaught>, <thort> or <thawt> without any of them being felt to be better than any other. In such a case, while variation is possible it will have little or no social meaning, since everyone is free to spell as they choose.

Although English does not have a formal regulatory institution comparable to French *Académie Française* and Italian *Accademia della Crusca*, there are several groups of individuals who, in our society, focus on ensuring that a professional Standard English orthography is followed, safeguarding us from a cultural and educational scenario where unruly spellings like those exemplified above become the norm (Condorelli, 2024: 3). Among the professional groups mentioned by Sebba (2007: 7–8), there are those of schoolteachers, professional writers and publishers. Spelling is a core unit of education in most schools, and, while it may not always be in the formal syllabus of every school, it takes up considerable time and energy for each schoolteacher to equip students with competence in English orthography (Sebba, 2007: 7; see Chapter 8, section 8.2). Likewise, orthographic practices from professional writers and publishers are scrutinised by the public, and criticism arises when the expected standard is not maintained. Misspellings found in newspapers and books never fail to encourage a portion of the most sensitive readers to write letters of complaint to publishers and news presses, reinforcing the general expectation that spellings should not be "allowed to slip" (Sebba, 2007: 7–8; see Chapter 6, section 6.2 on publishing standard rules).

Horobin's book takes a complementary stance to addressing the question of why correct English orthography plays an important role in society, giving more examples about the reasons why avoiding spelling mistakes is deemed important. The author explains, for example, that spelling errors on a commercial website may induce prospective customers to decide that the website is not trustworthy, just like emails which land our inbox written in unusual spellings have a higher chance of being identified as spam (Horobin, 2013: 4–5). At the same time, the author suggests, irregularity in English spelling is not necessarily always to be condemned as a sign of fraudulence, nor should it be used as a means to measure an individual's intelligence. After all, Horobin argues (2013: 3), one may be a very intelligent, highly educated person and still not be a proficient speller; likewise, one may be an excellent speller and still not rank at all among the brightest people on the planet – if creating such a ranking were indeed possible.

While using 'excellent' orthography may be a subjective desideratum, spelling irregularities are widespread objects of interest among many scholars engaging in sociolinguistics. The reason why orthographic variation has a role in sociolinguistic discourse is that standardisation is understood, through the lens of sociolinguistics, as a complex historical phenomenon deriving from non-linear mechanisms of regularisation, involving apparently counterintuitive patterns of individual spelling features and words. These counterintuitive patterns are sometimes considered 'standard' in their own time, even if they might differ from our present-day usage and could be mistaken for the product of carelessness. Examples include the forms *doe* and *goe*, which were common for 'do' and 'go' between the sixteenth and the early seventeenth centuries in England; likewise, *enough*, *inough* and *ynough* were all equally acceptable spellings before the 1580s, when *enough* became more common (examples from Basu, 2016: 180–182; Condorelli, 2022: 66–67).

Spellings such as those for 'do', 'go' and 'enough', therefore, have a long history of conflicted change and development (see Condorelli, 2022: 24). An anecdote discussed in Condorelli (2022: 146–147) with reference to sixteenth- and seventeenth-century English orthography may be useful as an additional example, and as a neat way of expanding on some of the spellings discussed with connection to graphotactics in Chapter 4 (section 4.3). The uses of the graphemes <i> and <j> in word-initial position to indicate /dʒ/ in words such as *Jesus*, in particular, became common in English between the 1620s and 1640s. The process of standardisation for these two graphemes was the result of changes occurring on the graphetic level in typographic and stylistic conventions, which saw a more sustained use of the roman typeface among London printers. Before the 1620s, a different custom involving two different communities of practice (Protestants and Catholics) was in place, which reflected the widespread view that the spelling *Iesus* was primarily 'Protestant', since black-letter (which is sometimes also known as 'Gothic'), most frequently used among Protestants, did not accommodate for the use of <j> word-initially. Conversely, *Jesus* was normally regarded as a 'Catholic' spelling, commonly associated with the roman typeface, where the use of <i> word-initially was indeed allowed (see Condorelli, 2022: 145–149).

The enforcement of the typographic rules explained above had an effect on large-scale spelling practices, to such an extent that the use of word-initial <i> in words like *Iesus* was becoming increasingly more frequent by the early seventeenth century in England. However, when these long-established expectations stemming from religious ideology ceased to exist, as a result of the Thirty Years' War (1618–1648) and the English Civil War (1642–1651), word-initial <i> and <j> lost their respective semiotic connotations. Favoured by the need to print books and pamphlets more quickly and to conform with Continental printing practices, where the roman typeface was becoming popular, word-initial <i> and <j> set out on a new journey towards standardisation, which eventually led to the conventions that we use today for the two word-initial graphemes in Standard English orthography (see Condorelli, 2022: 145–149).

Examples of orthographic standardisation where a drift from an earlier convention to a new arrangement occurs – such as that just described for word-initial <i> and <j> – follow a process of development formally known as *linguistic change.* According to Labov's sociolinguistic theory (1994), there are two ways in which linguistic change can take place: from 'above' and from 'below'. Changes *from above* normally occur by influence of "the dominant social class" (Labov, 1994: 78). Changes from above also happen "with full awareness", in the sense that they are intentionally introduced, for example, in order to mark a distinction between social classes, and "more frequently in formal styles" (Sairio and Palander-Collin, 2012: 630). Changes *from below*, however, "begi[n] in the vernacular", may arise from "any social class", and are "barely noticed until [they near] completion" (Sairio and Palander-Collin, 2012: 630–631).

The example of word-initial <i> and <j> represents an excellent way to show how the interaction between change from above and from below had an effect on the agreed norms for the two graphemes. Up until the early seventeenth century, book censorship, consciously regulated by an elite of powerful religious individuals based in London, was a key instrument for ensuring that the patterns of usage of word-initial <i> and <j> in black-letter and roman conformed to expected religious connotations (Condorelli, 2022: 146). As a result of the civil wars, the new system of using word-initial <i> and <j> gained momentum, more or less from below, as a joint effort from a large number of printers, both old and new, who no longer had to respond to the authority of government censorship and felt free to adopt what they believed were the most convenient typographic conventions (Condorelli, 2022: 148).

Examples of spelling developments such as those discussed so far, stemming from a selection of different types of contrasting spelling features, are quite frequent in written English, and undoubtedly make English orthography, and its connection to vocabulary, a fascinating yet methodologically challenging topic. The types of orthographic variation resulting from contrasting processes of change can be systematically approached, following Rutkowska and Rössler's sociolinguistic method (2012: 217–219), via six different categories: diachronic, diatopic, diaphasic, diastratic, diasituative, and aesthetic variants. Diachronic variants are the result of the coexistence of old and new orthographic arrangements, for example *hiccup* vs. *hiccough* and *jail* vs. *gaol*, though sometimes it may be difficult to identify which of the two variants is the oldest. Diatopic variants are the product of geographical variation, most typically the difference between American and British English in words like *color* vs. *colour* and *theater* vs. *theatre* (examples from Rutkowska and Rössler, 2012: 217).

Diaphasic variants reflect an individual writer's extent of orthographic variation during the course of his or her life and therefore include a wide range of idiosyncrasies. Diastratic and diasituative variants depend, respectively, on the writer's social communities, and the changing registers and genres of the texts where orthography is used. While examples of diastratic variants vary depending on the writer's social circumstances, diasituative variants include, for example, *program* vs. *programme*, which, in British English, are used, respectively, in the context of computers and to indicate a range of planned activities (examples from Rutkowska and Rössler, 2012: 218). Aesthetic variants are, much like diaphasic and diastratic variants, difficult to pinpoint with practical examples as they frequently depend on individual choices made in order to attract the reader's attention or to respond to a particular stylistic canon (Rutkowska and Rössler, 2012: 218–219).

All of the types of sociolinguistic variants described above are informed extensively by historical evidence, to such an extent that most of our current sociolinguistic understanding of English orthography cannot be removed from its historical context. The important place that historical sociolinguistics holds in our understanding of English orthography has encouraged the production of book-length introductions to historical sociolinguistics (e.g. McColl Millar, 2012) and major edited collections in historical sociolinguistics (Hernández-Campoy and Conde Silvestre, eds, 2012), which devote chapter-long contributions to English orthography. McColl Millar's introduction provides an overview of sociolinguistic theory and empirical methods, including micro- and macro-scale approaches to understanding historical variation, standardisation and language contact. Hernández-Campoy and Conde Silvestre's handbook, instead, presents theoretical frameworks, methodologies and case studies which marry together some of the most traditional approaches and more experimental outlooks on historical sociolinguistic issues.

The socio-historical linguistic reasoning for studying orthography in various parts of both of the key texts mentioned above is based on the idea that the ability to detect a standard form is more objectively evident in spelling than it is through other levels of historical linguistic analysis such as grammar and pronunciation (Trousdale, 2010: 13; compare Coulmas, 2013: 8, mentioned earlier in this section with reference to present-day spelling). In this context, orthographic standardisation, the collective diachronic effort to reach a standard, is intended as a socio-historical attempt to accomplish a level of uniformity and predictability that makes the system logical and intuitive (Görlach, 1990 [1988]: 14).

These socio-historical linguistic insights into studying standardisation in English orthography are best integrated, in my opinion, with perspectives from palaeography and bibliography. Let us briefly focus on palaeography first. Defined by the *Oxford Dictionary of Literary Terms* as "[t]he study and deciphering of old manuscripts" (Baldick, 2015: 263), palaeography focuses extensively on studying conventions in the making of letterforms and abbreviations, and how these defined individual writing communities, such as those of scribes. The connection between standardisation and palaeography consists in the idea that handwritten orthography often provided a baseline for some of the conventions that eventually became codified in printing. Beyond its immediate connection with printing, palaeography offers opportunities to appreciate the balance between variability and predictability in individual hands, across different textual contexts.

Among some of the most useful resources for those approaching palaeography for the first time, *Reading the Past* (Hoskin et al., 2001) offers valuable perspectives on sixteenth- and seventeenth-century handwriting, showcasing examples of common letterforms and abbreviations in the context of manuscript facsimiles. Another useful resource, available at the time of writing this textbook, is the online tutorial on palaeography published on The National Archives (2023), created in collaboration with the School of Library, Archive, and Information Studies (SLAIS) at University College London. This resource provides an interactive, step-by-step guide on how to approach orthographic features in handwriting, beginning with understanding the background history of the document under analysis, moving on to instructions on how to transcribe a document correctly (for example, using square brackets to signal abbreviated letters which have been expanded into their full spelling form) and how to identify single penstrokes in cursive handwriting, which is notoriously difficult to read (i.e. count how many penstrokes are visible to the naked eye in a given word and then leverage on that information to guess the word, drawing on sentence context). The National Archives tutorial also provides useful examples of some of the most frequent types of abbreviations found in handwritten English between 1500 and 1800, including suspensions (e.g. *M.* for 'majesty'), omissions (e.g. *demād* for 'demand' and *commissōn* for 'commission'), abbreviations (e.g. a 'p' with a horizontal bar crossing its tail to indicate the spelling 'per', in words such as 'person') and superscript letters (e.g. *w*^{t} for 'with') (examples from The National Archives, 2023).

7.2 Bibliographic perspectives

According to Gaskell (1972: 1), bibliography is "[t]he study of books as material objects". Building on Greg's definitions (1966: 75–88, 207–225, 239–266), Gaskell adds on the same page that bibliography is also "the science of the transmission of literary documents [...] their production and reproduction". Following Gaskell's footsteps, Bland (2010: 1) adds that bibliography encourages us to see handwritten and printed artefacts as "processes of communication in which meaning is made through the relationship between signs, structures, and materials".

The connection between bibliography and sociolinguistics may be identified as one of mutually complementary benefits. The ways in which literary documents are produced and transmitted, both in the present and the past, are influenced by the sociolinguistic contexts surrounding their creation. Conversely, sociolinguistic developments are sometimes conveyed through and devised for use in various textual contexts. To briefly return to the example of word-initial <i> and <j> discussed in section 7.1, for instance, there is a close correlation between the types of texts produced during the time in which the spelling changes took place and the socio-historical events motivating the production of these documents. Pamphlets, in particular, had a large influence on changing the English book market and production strategy in the mid-seventeenth century, due to their sheer quantity and popularity. Pamphlets were small booklets marketed in a way that was widely accessible: thanks to their format and size, they were relatively cheap, which means that they attracted the attention of many, including those who were less confident readers (see Condorelli, 2022: 143, 148). Due to their popularity, these texts became a key vehicle through which revolutionary ideas were spread during the English Civil War (1642–1651). Among the many ways in which the sentiment of political revolution was expressed in pamphlets, spelling change of the type discussed for word-initial <i> and <j> was one particularly connected to confessional turmoil and political power.

For students interested in English orthography, bibliographic perspectives of this kind are especially important, as writing only exists in textual contexts. In particular, English orthography is indirectly affected by textual constraints, or it actively contributes to creating textual features – or indeed both concurrently. For example, English orthography can be affected by textual limitations when margins require words placed near the right-hand side of the page to be separated between two lines by means of a hyphen (see also Chapter 5, section 5.1). Conversely, English orthography may actively contribute to creating textual features by helping readers to identify the beginning of new chapters, for example when the first letter, word or line in a new section is set in a larger size (see Chapter 6, section 6.2). On these premises, the intersection between English orthography and bibliography encourages researchers to investigate features immediately available to their eyes, which sometimes go unnoticed.[2]

In order to avoid problems arising from subjective interpretations of visual features, bibliographers have laid out a range of guidelines aimed at those interested in studying books. Since bibliography is primarily aimed at those working with historical books, the guidelines available

[2] Orthography alone, however, may also encourage purely linguistic analyses, as discussed in Part II of this textbook, with some references to issues involving syntax and semantics.

are more immediately applicable to language historians rather than those interested in present-day linguistics, though parallels between the two are possible. The Early Modern English era in particular (the sixteenth and the seventeenth centuries) has attracted interest from the largest number of scholars interested in bibliography, as this period shaped the English book industry and book market as we know them today. Within the context of English orthography, bibliographic insights are to be considered as separate from matters inherent to book history, which are more broadly concerned with the development of textual genres, the historical contexts underlying book production, and the correlation between texts, printers, authors, readers and literary patrons. Since these elements are also important for understanding the development of English orthography, especially from an historical perspective, they can be used, as will be discussed later in this chapter, as ways to inform explanatory accounts of spelling changes rather than as technical guidelines for studying evidence available in historical books.

Among the material available to those wishing to gain a better understanding of how to analyse an historical book, but with little or no prior knowledge on the topic, Gaskell's *A New Introduction to Bibliography* (1972) and Bland's *A Guide to Early Printed Books and Manuscripts* (2010) are the most thorough and accessible titles. Gaskell's manual provides details about the development of printing technology from its beginning, in the late fifteenth century, to the twentieth century, and explains the steps involved in book production over these centuries. The book is divided primarily into two parts: 'the hand-press period', which covers the period between 1500 and 1800, and 'the machine-press period', which focuses on the years between 1800 and 1950. The first part covers technical details involving the making of printing types[3] (including the chronological development of fonts), the process of typesetting, paper production (including the analysis of all the variables characterising paper, such as colour, fibre quality and manufacture), and the process of imposition, which entailed arranging paper in a way that made folding efficient, and minimised waste and errors. The book also describes how paper sheets were 'pressed' in order to be printed, the ways in which the printed material was left to dry once it was printed, the binding process, and how various decorations and illustrations (including relief blocks and intaglio plates) were implemented into the printing process. The second part of the book, focused on the machine-press period, discusses

[3] Printing types are three-dimensional metal-based letters used in moveable type technology (Gaskell, 1972: 5, 9).

the technological, organisational and trade-related advances made from the earliest decades of modern-technology printing.

Bland's manual integrates the information provided in Gaskell's volume by focusing in greater detail on various techniques of bibliographical identification and description of early printed books, which are only mentioned in passing by Gaskell (1972: 311–360). The book also devotes generous attention to manuscripts, discussing the close pragmatic correlations existing between them and printed books. Bland (2010: 154) explains, for example, how a text may have originally existed in oral form, before going through stages of untidy drafting, fair copying (often produced by professional copyists rather than the actual text authors), and how the finished product may have existed in different iterations before being distributed either as a handwritten manuscript or for use in a printing workshop as reference material for a printed copy. Another way in which Bland's book adds to Gaskell's manual is by integrating technical descriptions about manuscript and book production with the physical and cultural history of books as material objects. As the author argues, this approach enables scholars to indentify contextual similarities and differences in production practices across centuries with reference to, for example, the switch from black-letter to roman, the change from the use of marginal notes to footnotes, and the development "from single-volume folio collections to multi-volume octavo sets" (Bland, 2010: 5).

Some of the most relevant guidelines for orthographic discourse available in the two manuals discussed above include, for instance, those inherent to analysing paper and printing type (see Gaskell, 1972: 9–39, 57–77, 207–230, 283–288; Bland, 2010: 22–48, 116–121). Let us begin with paper, though the vagaries of its production ran in parallel with the strategies which took shape in printing workshops for the use and distribution of printing type. Sheets of paper from between the fifteenth to the seventeenth centuries are particularly interesting to bibliographers, because, especially at the early stages of printing in England, paper was produced, according to Bland (2010: 25), in small quantities using wire moulds. The rudimentary methods used for making paper mean that it is possible to trace a history of the moulds used for individual batches of paper and their watermarks. Due to their continued use, changes in the types of trays used for papermaking, and the interruptions in the production cycles that any repairs or replacements caused, can be tracked down and used to identify historical texts (Bland, 2010: 26). Moreover, as Bland explains (2010: 26), watermarks "encode the place of origin, the mill that made the paper, on what tray it was made, and when it was made". In bibliographic work, watermarks associated with individual texts and printers provide precious clues about who produced the paper, which stocks the paper produced belonged to, and the approximate age of the sheets on which a given text is printed (Bland, 2010: 26).

In addition to providing contextualising evidence on specific texts or printers for individual orthographic case studies, paper analysis is also valuable from larger-scale, quantitative perspectives on manufacturing changes. During the first two centuries since the invention of printing (c. 1500–1700), paper sheet formats mainly included, in decreasing order of size, folio (the standard size of a single sheet of paper), quarto (the fourth part of a folio), octavo (the eighth part of a folio) and duodecimo (the twelfth part of a folio). As a result of a series of economic decisions made over time in order to cut down book production costs, books were printed in sheets of increasingly smaller sizes, so that folio and quarto-sized books were often replaced by octavo and duodecimo editions (Shaw, 2007: 222; van Vliet, 2007: 247). Texts printed in these increasingly smaller books would have followed, one may logically assume, the same fate, being shrunk and squashed to fit in the space available.

In a pilot study recently conducted by Tyrkkö (2017b: 100), the author explored ways in which known large-scale patterns of diachronic simplification, such as those expressed above with regard to paper size, overlap with changes in the appearance of written English. Drawing on digital facsimiles of medical texts from the sixteenth and seventeenth centuries, Tyrkkö (2017b: 109) quantitatively demonstrated the presence of a steady reduction in the number of letters printed over the period under scrutiny. While the number of letters used declines over time, however, this steady decrease does not correlate with a lesser use of paper, which means that printers actually made, over time, a conscious decision to create books with "lighter, less blocky typefaces, as well as toward allowing more space between lines" (Tyrkkö, 2017b: 112). In a follow-up study (2017a: 103–104), the author found connections between spelling standardisation and the reduction of text and additional decorative features in Early Modern English books' title pages, suggesting, based on these close correlations, that bibliographic and orthographic levels of analysis should be conducted together more frequently.

Let us now move on to some basic bibliographic guidelines for analysing printing type, which inform our understanding of historical spelling in printed English. Gaskell (1972: 9) provides a systematic framework for understanding sixteenth- and seventeenth-century printing types, which also includes the identification of elements of three-dimensional metal letter shapes. Examples include the *baseline*, which is the imaginary horizontal line on which all letters normally stand, and which usually corresponds to a line on a page; the *x-height*, which refers to the height of the physical letter *x* and is taken as a reference point for measuring average character height; the *ascender*, which is the part of a letter which stretches above the x-height, such as the top portion of the physical letter *f*; and the *descender*, which is the section of a letter which stretches below the x-height, such as the lower portion of the physical letter *y*. A more systematic understanding of individual elements of a metal letter shape allows students of English orthography to add more layers of graphetic interpretations to the analysis of factors underlying English spelling change and standardisation.

In light of the description provided above, let us revisit again the example of word-initial <i> and <j> discussed in section 7.1. As mentioned in Condorelli (2022: 142), the turn of the seventeenth century saw a change in typesetting habits, whereby printers began to rely on spaces of different widths, depending on the letters of the alphabet used at the ends of each individual word. Although typesetters (also known as compositors) would likely not have had such a rigorous understanding of elements of a metal typeface like that provided by Gaskell, especially since they often delegated the job of making types to type foundries, they would have had, in any case, a sufficient practical understanding of the visual appearance of letter shapes. Compositors would have drawn on their experience-based knowledge in order to make deliberate choices about which types to use and when.

Letters with an ascender, such as <f>, especially when used at the end of a word (e.g. *turf*), were usually followed by a relatively long space, in order to prevent the ascender from appearing too closely to the following word. However, when a <j> was used as the first letter of the following word (e.g. *just*), a shorter space would normally be required, since the descender of <j> stretched out on the page longer (albeit infinitesimally) than than a letter without a descender (Condorelli, 2022: 142). Having a more predictable correlation between consonants/vowels and graphemes in the graphemic pair discussed above (word-initial <j> = /dʒ/ and word-initial <i> = vowels) would have allowed typesetters to predict more accurately how many printing types to purchase for a given project. It would also have allowed them to manipulate the wording of a sentence in order to flexibly find vocabulary that fit with the (sometimes small) number of letters and spaces available during each printing run (Mosley, 2009: 177; Condorelli, 2022: 143).

The shift from one standard to another in the uses of word-initial <i> and <j> in English orthography is even more remarkable if considered within the context of the material limitations existing in the early printing industry in England (which is where bibliography meets book history). Given the extent of manual labour necessary for printing a book, early printing workshops were engaged with relatively few projects, as evidenced by the historical records of book production. As discussed in Condorelli (2022: 55), the years 1500–1509 saw 439 English-language books coming from England, which was already a peak number compared to the quantity of books printed during the neighbouring years; only in the years 1650–1659 did a sharp spike in book production occur (16,523 books in total) (Raymond, 2011: 2). In addition, printing workshops were staffed by people with a small selection of roles: according to Howard-Hill (2006: 19), sixteenth- and seventeenth-century workshops were only attended by a master printer, typesetters and apprentices. While master printers took most managerial and finance-related decisions, and typesetters were in charge of supervising the various processes of printing, the physical printing labour fell frequently on the apprentices' shoulders. These were usually young boys who received little schooling prior to their service. Even the most promising apprentices, who were given multiple typesetting projects, frequently made compositorial mistakes.

At least until the end of the seventeenth century, the numbers of apprentices would have been higher than those appearing on public records. As stated in a report available in the Public Record Office (cited by Howard-Hill, 2006: 20), printers operating in London were, by the last decades of the seventeenth century, 198, "of whom 75 per cent were journeymen, 13 per cent masters, and 12 per cent apprentices" (Gaskell, 1972: 176). In reality, master printers were encouraged to hire as many apprentices as possible thanks to the fact that they received little to no pay and therefore provided virtually free labour (Howard-Hill, 2006: 19–20). Some of the newly hired apprentices were in charge of collecting individual types from their type cases, handing them over to the typesetter, and redistributing the used type back into their cases once the printing was done. This task took a great deal of cognitive effort on their part, as type was often distributed across cases in no self-intuitive order (Howard-Hill, 2006: 22). It is not difficult to imagine that the apprentices' mistakes often stifled not only orthographic standardisation in the books produced, but also reading comprehension among those who bought them. More insights into the cognitive aspects underlying the processes of reading and writing English orthography, of both the past and the present, are provided in Chapter 8.

Discussion Material

1. Why do you think that sociolinguistics has attracted a great deal of interest over the last few decades among students of linguistics?
2. Discuss, using your own words and examples, how historical spelling changes can inform our understanding of present-day English orthography.
3. What is it about historical sociolinguistics that makes it distinct from sociolinguistics and what are some of the most important points in common between the two?
4. Based on the information available in Gaskell's and Bland's manuals, what do you think are some other pieces of bibliographic information that are useful for those interested in studying the English writing system?
5. How do you think the book production industry will be affected by future technological advances?

Recommendations for Reading

Bland, Mark (2010), *A Guide to Early Printed Books and Manuscripts*, London: Wiley-Blackwell.

Condorelli, Marco (2022), *Standardising English Spelling: The Role of Printing in Sixteenth and Seventeenth-Century Graphemic Developments*, Studies in English Language, Cambridge: Cambridge University Press, pp. 127–149.

Gaskell, Philip (1972), *A New Introduction to Bibliography*, Oxford: Oxford University Press.

McColl Millar, Robert (2012), *English Historical Sociolinguistics*, Edinburgh: Edinburgh University Press, pp. 1–16, 43–76.

Trousdale, Graeme (2010), *An Introduction to English Sociolinguistics*, Edinburgh: Edinburgh University Press, pp. 11–14, 41–75.

8 Psychology and literacy

8.1 Psychology of reading

The previous chapter provided a discussion of the overlap between English orthography on one hand, and sociolinguistics and bibliography on the other hand. The first half of the chapter argued that orthography plays an important role in sociolinguistic discourse about variation and standardisation, since orthographic features frequently work as variables which signal broader social and historical events. The second part of the chapter continued to focus on standardisation by offering an overview of bibliography and book history, and discussing their relevance in the history of English orthography. Examples of bibliographic topics that were deemed particularly helpful are those involving the study of paper and printing type. This chapter continues the conversation about topics situated at the intersection between the English writing system and other interdisciplinary areas of academic enquiry, delving into a discussion about key elements from the psychology of reading and literacy studies.

The psychology of reading, the area of academic enquiry concerned with "the psychological processes that underlie the practice of reading" (Kennedy, 2018: xvi), is connected in several ways to bibliography and, more broadly, book history. Both within the context of English studies and beyond, historians and psychologists of reading have an interest in the relationship between individuals and written texts. Moreover, they both ask questions aimed at understanding the relationship between the written form and the message delivered in writing, including the extent to which comprehension is attained through textual layout design (Elfenbein, 2006: 485–486). Both book historians and psychologists of reading frequently seek to understand the extent to which a reader's educational background affects his or her reading performance, and, in turn, the degree to which texts help the reader to achieve a higher level of literacy (see also section 8.2). The assumption from which both book historians and psychologists of reading depart is that readers have a role in shaping literacy and textual reception, and historical texts in turn actively contribute to shaping reading audiences (Elfenbein, 2006: 486). English orthography is the medium through which both goals are attained, as well as the means through which strategic developments are detected.

Against this backdrop, book historians and psychologists of reading often find themselves pursuing complementary research routes, which depart from patterns available in the written text. On one hand, psychologists of reading focus on identifying widespread text-decoding methods used by contemporary readers and the ways in which information absorbed from contemporary readers is stored mentally. On the other hand, book historians look for cognitive patterns behind the process of book-making and marketing, enquiring what historical readers looked for in each text under analysis, and how the socio-cultural contexts in which a given group of readers was embedded forged the expected reading approach for individual texts (Elfenbein, 2006: 484–485). While the goals above are interdependent, and scholars from either areas may draw on the other field to inform their studies, differences between psychological and historical research may arise from the fact that psychologists of reading usually focus on relatively simple texts, while historians, especially those interested in reading, might engage with "exceptionally intricate texts, like novels" (Elfenbein, 2006: 484–485). The analysis of historical fiction in particular has a higher likelihood to show evidence for the existence of unusual reading strategies (as intended by the author and as applied by readers), and, depending on the overall goals of the work of fiction, it might encourage one to question the definition of 'successful' vs. 'unsuccessful' reading experiences (Elfenbein, 2006: 485–486).

Notwithstanding the existence of complementary research routes, book history and the psychology of reading may feel, as argued by Elfenbein (2006: 484), like two completely different worlds. While departing from some of the same empirical questions, practitioners and scholars involved in either research groups often end up using "contrasting methods of defining, analyzing, investigating, and evaluating" concepts and data stemming from their respective research programmes (Elfenbein, 2006: 484). The practical divergences existing between book historians and psychologists of reading entail the fact that members from each of the two disciplines become engaged in an increasingly inward-looking research cluster, and that any interactions between the humanist and the scientific sides of the study of books and reading must be facilitated by explicit interdisciplinary endeavours. Examples of such endeavours include the organisation of conferences with broad topics, the compilation of interdisciplinary edited volumes and the formation of an educational setting such as a university faculty or research team with an interest in fostering connections between the two areas.

While notions from bibliography and book history are normally not explicitly addressed as a topic of interest in publications that concern the psychology of reading, and vice versa, there are examples, albeit rare, of studies in English orthography that touch upon both areas concurrently, while also addressing sociolinguistic research questions. An example is that of a chapter written by Sönmez (2000), where similarities and divergences in spellings between Lady Brilliana Harley (1600–1643) and of the Duke of Newcastle (1592–1676) are investigated, with a view of finding out whether the woman's and the man's non-standard spellings in their respective manuscript texts are perceived as equal or whether spellings from one of the two "look more wrong than others" (Sönmez, 2000: 409). The author is interested in answering the question of whether there is a degree of markedness in our understanding, as present-day readers and students of English orthography, of non-standard spelling, and whether social or literacy variables affect such perceptions (compare the statements made in Chapter 7, section 7.1 regarding counterintuitive spelling patterns). In order to understand how readers may be affected in their perception of non-standard spellings, Sönmez (2000: 426) draws on psycholinguistic research focusing on reading strategies of both children in the process of learning how to read and high-literacy adults (e.g. Huxford et al., 1992; Beauvillain, 1996). On this basis, the author suggests that the first chunk of a word, including the first letter of a word or its prefix, is perceived as more important than all the other components of the same word. Consequently, Harley's spelling, which features a larger number of non-standard choices found especially word-initially (e.g. *a bowte*, *all ways*, *be come*, *in joy*, *for giue*, *to morowe* and *will coeme*) is perceived, perhaps mistakenly, as more irregular than the Duke of Newcastle's spelling (examples from Sönmez, 2000: 425–426).

The author also discusses additional findings from the psychology of reading in order to draw attention to the fact that readers normally construct "an orthographic image for words they have encountered frequently" (Crowder and Wagner, 1992: 82, as quoted in Sönmez, 2000: 430). These orthographic 'images' may be formed regardless of whether standard or non-standard forms are used in a given text. To support this claim, Sönmez (2000: 430) draws on psycholinguistic findings from Campbell (1987) in order to argue that both standard and non-standard spellings may become accepted as familiar in the readers' mental lexicon if they occur frequently enough. As a result, idiosyncratic spelling forms, namely non-standard spellings which do not appear regularly and are therefore not stored in readers' minds as familiar spelling forms, may stand out more markedly as incorrect during the reading process. To address the fact that Harley's spellings are more idiosyncratic in nature than the Duke of Newcastle's, psychological findings, the author argues, clearly help with explaining the differences in the degree of markedness existing between the woman's and the man's spelling features, despite the fact that the extent of non-standard spellings between the two is, on the whole, relatively similar (Sönmez, 2000: 430–431).

Albeit less extensively than in Sönmez, findings from work in the psychology of reading are also discussed in Condorelli (2022: 210), with reference to the standardisation of <ea> and <oa> in English orthography between the sixteenth and the seventeenth centuries. In that book, it is argued that, while these two digraphs follow a straightforward quantitative pattern of development, across both high- and low-frequency words, their phonemic indications remained quite vague during these two centuries. In particular, frequently occurring words like *heart* could be pronounced, in the late sixteenth century, with an /a/ or an /ɛ/, while the vowel pronunciation of *hear* swung between /ɛ:/ and /i:/ over the late sixteenth and the early seventeenth centuries. Likewise, vowels in words such as *boar* and *board* could be ambiguously pronounced with an /ɔ:/ or with an /o:/ (Lass, 1999: 109–112; Condorelli, 2022: 198–199).[1] While these inconsistencies could initially bring into question why the spellings mentioned above became more widely used despite the fact that they presented challenges for both readers and writers, a more up-to-date version of Sönmez's psycholinguistic claim made above – though following the same core concept – is drawn on in the book in order to find a solution to this dilemma.

As discussed in research focused on reading strategies (Perfetti and Hart, 2002; Perfetti, 2007), reading efficiency is achieved, first of all, by making the spelling form of each word consistent, while the possible pronunciations underlying each word, that is to say, the graphemic-phonemic correspondences in the spelling of each word, only have secondary influence on reading performance (Condorelli, 2022: 210). Consistency in the uses of <ea> and <oa> in sixteenth- and seventeenth-century English from a visual perspective, on the word level, as opposed to the phonemic level, was, it is argued in the book, especially important, because of the fragmented way in which books were printed

[1] There are, of course, further issues underlying these otherwise simplified pronunciations, mostly to do with evidence and causes of variation.

at the time. Since early modern printers could only typeset a small number of lines at a time, they would usually work with small, out-of-context portions of text, and were therefore encouraged to prioritise more visual, context-independent approaches to typesetting their text portions systematically (Gaskell, 1972: 42; Condorelli, 2022: 206–207). Additionally, establishing and following fixed in-house word spelling rules, it is maintained in Condorelli's book, would have been easier for typesetters than ensuring that words with the same vowel pronunciations were spelled consistently, since typesetters often migrated, in order to take up printing jobs, from different corners of England and from abroad, carrying different vowel pronunciations with them (Howard-Hill, 2006: 19; Condorelli, 2022: 205, 210).

Although "visual word recognition might appear to be a deceptively simple task involving pattern recognition" (Yap and Rickard Liow, 2016: 453), recent psycholinguistic research has shown that, beyond the remits of manuscript writing and the historical printing workshop, there are more levels of complexity to the task of reading present-day English – some of which overlap with orthography and phonology. Table 8.1 summarises some of the most relevant findings discussed in Yap and Rickard Liow (2016) with reference to English orthography, and especially the idea that word recognition is facilitated not only by visual consistency, as stated so far, but also by the extent to which a given word is similar, orthographically and phonologically, to other words present in English vocabulary. The higher the number of orthographic and phonological neighbours present for a given word in English vocabulary, the more likely it will be for that word to be recognised by the reader more quickly than other idiosyncratic word forms.

Findings on individual word recognition processes are embedded in wider discussions about the relationship between English orthography and text comprehension, which are summarised in handbooks on cognitive aspects of reading (e.g. Snowling and Hulme, 2005; Reisberg, 2013; Pollatsek and Treiman, 2015) and, to some extent, introductory volumes on the psychology of reading (e.g. Schwanenflugel and Flanagan Knapp, 2016; Kennedy, 2018). Among the material available in these collections, Kintsch and Rawson's chapter from *The Science of Reading: A Handbook* (2005) and Gernsbacher and Kaschak's chapter from the *Oxford Handbook of Cognitive Psychology* (2013) are particularly useful, within the context of this textbook, for illustrating the steps involved in text comprehension, and how these intersect with elements in the English writing system.

Gernsbacher and Kaschak's chapter explains that there are different levels on which meaning is constructed through a text, the most basic

Table 8.1 The length effect (from Yap and Rickard Liow, 2016: 456–457)

Effect of orthographic similarity in individual word recognition The so-called *length effect* consists of the fact that words with a longer spelling form, such as *caterpillar*, are generally recognised by the reader more slowly than words with a shorter spelling form, for instance *cat*. The comparatively slower response to word recognition is owed to the fact that the orthographic form of a longer word is less likely associated with other words with similar pronunciations. The word *caterpillar*, in particular, has a fairly unique form and pronunciation (/ˈkætəpɪlə/), while the word *cat* (/kæt/) looks and sounds like a few other words in English vocabulary, for instance *hat*, *cot* and *cap* (/hæt/, kɒt/ and /kæp/) (examples from Yap and Rickard Liow, 2016: 456–457). Similarities of the type explained above are measured using a system called *orthographic neighbourhood size*, which, in Yap and Rickard Liow's words (2016: 457), "is defined by the number of orthographic neighbours a word possesses, where neighbour is defined as any word that can be obtained by substituting a single letter of a target word". The orthographic similarity metric is sometimes used, in the analysis system explained by Yap and Rickard Liow (2016: 456–457), in conjunction with the *phonological neighbourhood size*, which "reflects a target word's number of phonological neighbours (i.e., words created by substituting a single phoneme) so the neighbours of *gate* include *hate*, *get* and *bait*" (Yap and Rickard Liow, 2016: 457). The higher the number of orthographic and phonological 'neighbours' to the word being recognised by the reader, the shorter the response times to word recognition, which means that similarly looking and sounding words facilitate, rather than inhibit, the act of reading.

of which entails readers working out what each orthographic unit in the text signifies, the ways in which these units go together to represent vocabulary, and how they interrelate to provide grammatical order (Gernsbacher and Kaschak, 2013: 462). This first level of comprehension is sometimes known as the *surface level* and allows readers to understand the text exactly as intended in writing, word by word (Gernsbacher and Kaschak, 2013: 464). More complex levels, however, require readers to "establish a [mental] representation to keep track of the events [...]" being narrated in a text, "to be aware of the goals of the characters, and so on" (Gernsbacher and Kaschak, 2013: 463). While the role of orthography on the more basic level of text comprehension is more immediately connected to the steps followed by a learner during literacy acquisition, and focuses on establishing graphemic-phonemic correspondences (further described in section 8.2), more complex layers of text comprehension are usually achieved through other orthographic cues, such as paragraph and page structures, understanding white space distribution strategies, and assessing content-signalling material such as titles, subtitles, abstracts and side notes.

Two complex layers of text comprehension are normally distinguished in text comprehension theory, both of which can be accessed through a variety of linguistic strategies, including syntactic, semantic and orthographic. The first of these two is the *textbase*, which is a "propositional representation of the ideas explicitly stated in the text" (Gernsbacher and Kaschak, 2013: 464). The textbase is the level at which textual meaning, rather than just the superficial words or sentences, is constructed at the micro level (microstructure) and at the macro level (macrostructure). Microstructure construction occurs through the creation of prepositions, chunks of meaning created from each individual sentence; macrostructure construction, however, consists of the building of meaning in larger sections of text than individual sentences, such as whole sections or the full text (Kintsch and Rawson, 2005: 210–211). As argued by Kintsch and Rawson (2005: 211), the textbase level of comprehension, albeit more complex, is still insufficient for full understanding, especially if readers aim to get a thorough and more comprehensive understanding of the text.

An even more complete understanding of the text occurs through the second of the more complex layers of text comprehension, known as the *situational level*, which deals with the ultimate interpretation of the text – beyond what is said on the surface. The situational level is described by Gernsbacher and Kaschak (2013: 465) as "an amalgam of information that is contained in the textbase and information that has been retrieved from the comprehender's general store of world knowledge (Kintsch, 1988)". At this stage, the authors continue, readers have to actively use their personal world knowledge in order to give the text full meaning and to fill in the gaps left by individual sentences, arriving at a level of meaning that is not immediately available in a given text (Gernsbacher and Kaschak, 2013: 463). To draw on the example given by Kintsch and Rawson (2005: 211–213), the situational level allows a reader to understand a textbook description focused on 'the valves' not as a stand-alone mechanism but rather as a component of the circulatory system in the human heart. According to Zwaan et al. (1995), the situational level usually aims to find answers along five different parameters: protagonists ('who is the agent in the circumstances being narrated?'); time ('when are the events in question happening?'); space ('what geographical areas are shared among the individuals and objects involved in the events?'); causality ('which circumstances are the cause or the effect of which?'); and, finally, intentionality ('how relevant are the details being narrated to the protagonists' objectives?') (Gernsbacher and Kaschak, 2013: 465).

A number of relatively recent research papers illustrate the extent to which organisational elements in English orthography play an important role in assessing text comprehension within the framework explained above. In particular, a few studies led by McNamara (McNamara, 2001; McNamara and Kintsch, 1996; McNamara et al., 1996; O'Reilly and McNamara, 2007; McNamara et al., 2011) investigated the influence of *textual cohesion*, intended as the application of linguistic features which establish connections among adjacent components of a text, at the interplay between field-specific knowledge and comprehension accomplishment (McNamara et al., 2011: 233). The researchers involved in these studies altered target texts with the aim of achieving low-cohesion and high-cohesion outcomes, drawing, for example, on punctuation as a connective system, headers as topic indicators, and blank spaces as target areas for additional explanatory information. The results showed that those with little context-specific knowledge benefited more from a higher level of cohesion than those with more knowledge, as connective devices helped those readers to form a situational model in a way that would otherwise not have been possible with the unedited versions of the target texts (McNamara et al., 2011: 233). While these findings may strike one as somewhat expected, not all reading aids are helpful at all times: as evidenced by a study conducted on the influence of visual aids in text comprehension among pupils between seven and thirteen years of age (Seger et al., 2021), illustrations which appeared immediately after the portion of text that the images referred to actually hindered textbase comprehension, as they interrupted the process of textbase information construction.

8.2 Literacy studies

The references made to text comprehension at the end of section 8.1 are a convenient bridge to the second and last section of this chapter, focused on the intersection between literacy studies and the English writing system. Psychology of reading and literacy studies are clearly very closely connected. As argued by Bloome and Green (2015: 19), "literacy (reading and writing) has [...] been defined as a set of cognitive processes and skills". The authors go on to say that empirical work on literacy, particularly in relation to pedagogical education, has almost exclusively investigated the psychological framework underlying the process of literacy acquisition (Bloome and Green, 2015: 19–20). While this view has recently been updated with the idea that literacy is a skill that is "essentially social and situated in the interactions among people" (Bloome and Green, 2015: 20), the psycholinguistic aspects of literacy acquisition remain a staple in research overlapping pedagogy and English orthography.

The perspective that ultimately connects text comprehension with literacy acquisition is that stemming from pragmatics, an area of linguistic understanding which revolves around communicability (Cummins, 2019: 1). Pragmatics, specifically applied to the English writing system, entails not only the idea of encoding the meaning of written signs by the writer and decoding it by the reader as conventionally agreed in most communicative scenarios, but also accounting for the semantic role of exceptions to the existing rules, and how and why they take place (Cummins, 2019: 1–4). Pragmatics is to do with all the contextual information that gives a communicative scenario its true meaning: the lead-up to the written statement under analysis, the textual background in which it is situated, the reason why the statement is made at all, the knowledge available to the writer at the time of writing, and so on (Cummins, 2019: 5).

The pragmatic connection between the psychology of reading and literacy studies is one that ultimately encompasses the art of mastering the English writing system as a whole. Examining the cognitive requirements and abilities needed in order to learn how to read and write in literacy studies inevitably means accessing the pragmatic circumstances that enable complete meaning to be conveyed successfully across all its complex text comprehension levels (surface level > textbase > situational level). For example, the ability to understand a series of written statements, and the way in which punctuation is weaved around them, in their full ironic intent, requires, for readers, breaking down the logical signals and gaps left by punctuation (for example, by means of spaces, dashes or dots) and other cognitive-emotional cues (exclamation and question marks), among other linguistic elements, as strategies dictated by a specific writer, within the context of a specific text devised for a particular reading purpose.

Current empirical approaches aimed at investigating the two most important components of literacy – reading and writing – show that, while clearly connecting pragmaticists, sociolinguists, book historians, psychologists and literacy scholars, both components can also become a cause of deep divisions. Price (2004: 304), for example, affirms that reading encourages different empirical approaches depending on the researchers involved: for literary critics, for instance, the topic encourages case studies aimed at investigating readerly approaches to a given text or discussing theoretical interpretative methods; for historians, reading fosters research questions in cultural or intellectual history. These words echo those of Hall (1996: 169), who claimed before Price that reading can be an object of interest not only in "social history", "the history of education" and "the hermeneutics of interpretation", but also the history of the book as a material object and its relationship with those involved in producing and consuming the product. Research in recent years, however, has gone a long way in establishing helpful connections across the branches of intellectual enquiry discussed so far in this third part of this textbook. One of the most relevant contributions in this sense is that of a volume titled *Literary Acquisition and Social Context* (edited by Assink, 2014 [1994]), where the thread followed is that of the importance of socially induced learning in the overall process of literary acquisition, especially with reference to learning how to read.

A couple of chapters contained in that collection are particularly noteworthy with regard to the issues discussed here. In 'The role of social context in emergent literacy', Bus (2014 [1994)]) focuses on the fact that, in well-educated societies, literacy acquisition occurs before children are introduced to reading in school. Children acquire a foundational knowledge of key characteristics of reading in social contexts such as that of bedtime reading and home-based casual conversation, often under the mentorship of their own parents. Such foundational knowledge, it is argued by Bus (2014 [1994)]: 10), is built gradually following a "scaffolding" process, during which the parent guides the child through all those elements in the narrative that are above the early learner's comprehension skills while allowing the child to focus on aspects that are within the remits of the child's knowledge. As part of the process of learning, children are encouraged by their parents to begin noticing spelling forms, for example by associating the image of an ice-cream with the letter *i* (Bus, 2014 [1994)]: 12). The chapter also places emphasis on the consequences of the existence of a socially based pathway to early learning revolving around parents and children: good relationships between the parent and the child may be beneficial on the child's long-term relationship with reading (and, one may assume, also with English orthography), while bad relationships may reveal themselves to be detrimental (Bus, 2014 [1994)]: 10).

In 'Codes, connections, context and constructive processes: Integrating the Vygotskian and Lurian perspectives', Berninger (2014 [1994)]) explains that the social element of literacy acquisition can coexist with more traditional psycholinguistic views based on purely orthographic and phonological cues. In particular, Berninger points to the fact that components of the English writing system, such as individual letters, groups of letters and full-word spellings, and the sounds associated with them, have key roles in guiding the learning-how-to-read process (Berninger, 2014 [1994)]: 34–36). While these are well-known steps for learning how to read for both adults and children, whether and how they are followed depends, according to the author, on the educational strategy offered to the children and the environment in which learning occurs (Berninger, 2014 [1994)]: 40). If the social context encourages content-focused reading practices, young learners will follow this content-focused pathway; if the social context fosters linguistically oriented reading practices, young learners will use spelling and phonetic cues to learn how to read. Variables like vocabulary, text organisation and meaning, and they ways in which these are absorbed in the young learners' memory, will depend on the texts to which children are exposed (Berninger, 2014 [1994)]: 43). A more recent chapter on literacy acquisition provides further details about the processes identified by Berninger for learning how to read. In 'How children learn to read words', Ehri (2015) argues that learning to read occurs not only by connecting orthographic units with sounds and linking word forms to meanings, but also through memory. The author shows that memory retrieval is reinforced by exposure to as many sentence contexts as possible, which allows children to become prepared for complex orthographic, phonological and semantic scenarios.

Much like research on present-day issues in literacy acquisition, historical perspectives also offer insights into reading-based literacy acquisition through repetitive exposure. One such example is that of Nevalainen's (2012) chapter. In the final section of the chapter in particular (2012: 157), Nevalainen argues for the influence of the Bible, the most widespread, authoritative and politically charged book for many centuries in England, in shaping English orthography through reading-based learning activities. Editions such as the King James Bible (1611), Nevalainen argues, provided useful orthographic guidelines for the spelling changes that occurred in Older Scots between the sixteenth and the seventeenth centuries (Nevalainen, 2012: 158). Some of these guidelines were gradually absorbed by readers, who often held up the Bible as their sole fount of knowledge and their only opportunity for acquiring literacy. As a result, the Scottish spelling <quh> in words like *where* and *which*, for instance, was replaced by <wh> quite abruptly at the turn of the two centuries mentioned above, upon inspiration from the Bible (Devitt, 1989: 19; Nevalainen, 2012: 158).

Reading-based literacy acquisition activities also involved the Geneva Bible (1560), which was the first study bible published in English and was heavily used by readers of all ages and levels of education. The Geneva Bible's correlation with presumed levels of literacy among readers was studied by Molekamp (2006), who argues that, on the basis of handwritten evidence surviving on existing Geneva Bible copies, "readers can be seen using their bible as a site to improve their reading and writing" (Molekamp, 2006: 12). Among those who engaged with the book, some readers practised surface-level reading aimed not so much at understanding theological content, but rather at learning English by reproducing the same lines printed in the Bible in their own handwriting. Molekamp states that the British Library holds twelve copies of the Geneva Bible where evidence of such literacy-related activities is available, for example in the form of wobbly bible verse repetitions and shakily scribbled individual characters written to practise the English alphabet (Molekamp, 2006: 12).

"In one black letter quarto", the author argues, "the reader has copied out an italic minuscule alphabet in a shaky and messy hand, suggesting he or she is not proficient in handwriting. In another a child scrawls in a seventeenth-century italic hand, 'James Sparke His Book Colchester Essex Nearly 13 yeares of age wrote bad'" (Molekamp, 2006: 12). In order to uncover the meaning of all the examples encountered by the author, theoretical knowledge of the English writing system is helpful, as Bible copies feature notes appearing "often in poor handwriting, rough syntax and flawed orthography" (Molekamp, 2006: 9). For instance, an understanding of sixteenth- and seventeenth-century glyphs (see Chapter 4, section 4.2) for individual letters of the alphabet, and knowledge of graphotactic constraints (see Chapter 4, section 4.3) existing in English at the time, help with appreciating similarities among individual letters and establishing their graphemic values, as well as setting expectations for letter combinations within each individual word in English vocabulary.

The various functionalist approaches that the English writing system can have within the same historical text during the act of reading (that of providing biblical content vs. that of helping the reader to learn how to read, in the Geneva Bible example) point, once again, to the pragmatic aspect of linguistic analysis. Historical pragmatics departs from the same points of enquiry summarised for present-day pragmatics more broadly earlier in this book, while adding an historical, frequently diachronic component to writing system analysis. An excellent resource for students interested in exploring historical pragmatic aspects in the study of the English writing system is Jucker and Taavitsainen's *English Historical Pragmatics* (2013). While not focusing specifically on the English writing system, that textbook offers, for example, useful insights into methodologies that allow students with an interest in the English writing system to take "people and contexts into account" when approaching historical texts (Jucker and Taavitsainen, 2013: 32). Examples span from qualitative to corpus linguistics methods, which could address, from a reader's perspective, how orthographic features attempt to place a given text within a specific discourse and genre setting, and how they offer new meanings to individual words and sentences (Jucker and Taavitsainen, 2013: 33–34).[2]

While reading as a literacy acquisition practice has received some synergic attention from scholars working across some of the branches of knowledge discussed in this third part of the textbook, thus enabling some cohesive approaches, writing is perhaps an even more divisive area of empirically informed discussion, when connected to literacy studies. In literacy studies, English writing is an object of prescriptive concern for some, and a subject of more objective scientific investigation for others. Prescriptive remarks on the topic are those followed, for example, by Venezky (1999), Moats (2000) and Nicholson (2005), who agree on a series of milestones which should be followed in order to teach English orthography to children. The steps, summarised by Brown (2019: 227–229), are reorganised in Table 8.2 below in a way that is, it is hoped, most efficient for illustrative purposes. Milestones such as those identified in Brown's work are a testimony to the fact that prescriptive approaches to learning how to write are still thought, in English literacy studies, to be most effective when taught through explicit guidelines.

Examples of more objective, linguistic case studies into writing as an element of literacy studies are provided by Cook (2004: 124–138). A foundational study mentioned by Cook (2004: 124–125) within the section referenced above is that conducted by the National Foundation for Education Research (Brooks et al., 1993). In that study, "essays written by 1492 secondary school children in England at the two ages of 11 and 15 years" (Cook, 2004: 124) were investigated, with a view of understanding the frequency and type of spelling error occurring during the process of learning how to write. The quantitative results showed that, "[a]t the age of 11, only two children out of 10 had no mistakes; two out of 10 had five or more. By age 15, four children out of 10 had no mistakes; one out of 10 had five or more" (Cook, 2004: 124). The qualitative results, instead, revealed the following spelling errors (in this lightly modified quote from Cook, 2004: 124):

> insertion of extra letters, such as the <l> added to 'untill'; *omission* of letters, such as the <r> missing from 'occuring'; *substitution* of different letters, such as instead of <i> in 'definate'; *transposition* of two letters, such as <ei> for <ie> in 'freind'; *grapheme substitution* involving more than two

[2] From a writer's perspective, qualitative and corpus linguistics methods can illuminate ways in which punctuation and capitalisation, discussed separately in Part II from a theoretical perspective, came about to take pragmatic functions together in practice (e.g. indicating emotional stress in sentences such as 'I said stop. STOP!').

> letters but only a single cause, for example when an equivalent according to sound correspondence rules is substituted for the usual form, as in 'thort' for 'thought'.

The study, according to Cook (2004: 125), is limited in the extent to which it identifies error patterns, but still represents a helpful example of the close relationship between elements in the English writing system and the acquisition of English writing skills among children and teenagers.

In historical literacy research, writing has been studied, for example, to understand the spread of 'practical' literacy, that is to say, the skills needed to fulfil everyday writing needs (Ford, 1993: 22–23). According to Fox (2017: 136–137), research in signature mining in particular provides a great deal of information about gender-related differences in sixteenth- and seventeenth-century practical literacy in England: in 1500, 10 per cent of men were able to write their own full signature against 1 per cent of women; by 1558, when Queen Elizabeth rose to the throne of England, the same ability was shared by 20 per cent of men and 5 per cent of women; by 1642, which marks the beginning of the Civil War, it was shared by 30 per cent of men and 10 per cent of women (Fox, 2017: 136–137). Other signature-informed evidence, as provided by Hubbard (2015: 567), shows that,

> [o]f the 2,342 London women who marked, initialled, or signed their depositions for the London Consistory Court between 1570 and 1640, 15 percent wrote at least one initial and 10 per cent signed at least their first name, suggesting that at least a quarter of London women had at least begun learning how to read.[3]

Signature-informed evidence available in Cressy's work (1977), instead, provides details about the social class distribution of literacy. By the 1590s, the author argues (Cressy, 1977: 9–10), those belonging to the higher social strata, such as the working class, the gentry and those with clerical occupations in the diocese of Norwich, were all able to sign their full name. The percentages of those working in other occupations, however, varied: about 62 per cent of yeomen, 45 per cent of tradesmen,

[3] These facts need to be put into their historical context. Writing and reading are separate skills, which were often taught separately; the education of girls was often limited to reading only. This means that this evidence of how many women were able to write does not automatically reflect the numbers of those who were able to read, which may well have been much higher. The separation between reading and writing as two individual skills was perhaps perceived more strongly in the past than it is today and existed across different social classes, including higher classes.

Table 8.2 Milestone sequence for teaching English orthography (after Brown, 2019: 227–229)

Prescriptive remarks on writing as a topic in literacy studies

1) *Associating sound values*: gaining a general understanding of the fact that letters indicate sounds, and a general ability to distinguish consonants from vowels.
2) *Learning the alphabet*: being able to name every individual letter of the English alphabet.
3) *Matching letters to sounds*: learning how to associate letters of the alphabet with sounds.
4) *Distinguishing essential sound units*: identifying different sounds in English, especially vowels (e.g. /ʌ/ in *cup*, which needs to be perceived as different from /æ/ in *cap*).
5) *Learning short spelling forms and sounds*: writing words of the smallest and simplest structure, usually consisting in a vowel surrounded by two consonants on either side (e.g. *mum*, *bin* and *top*). A follow-up stage consists in writing words with a vowel surrounded by more than one consonant on either side (e.g. *street*).
6) *Learning complex consonant values*: grasping cases where two or three consonants do not indicate individual consonant sounds (e.g. <tch> in *match*). A follow-up stage is that of mastering, for instance, <oo> in *doom*, which represents one sound, /uː/, and <ea> in *leave*, which indicates /iː/.
7) *Using word-final e*: learning to write words like *phone* and *drone*, where word-final <e> indicates lengthening and <o> represents a diphthong.
8) *Using rhotacism vs. non-rhotacism*: understanding the relationship between vocalic sounds and <r> (*far*, /fɑː/, /fɑːɹ/).
9) *Writing multisyllabic words*: assembling words (e.g. *base* + *ball* in *baseball*) and mastering complexity (e.g. *purpose*).

   Manipulating vocabulary: using affixes and suffixes to change the meaning of basic nouns (e.g. *kind* vs. *unkind*).

and 13 per cent of husbandmen were capable of signing their full names by the 1590s. These percentage figures rose steadily up to the mid-seventeenth century for yeomen, tradesmen and husbandmen, though illiteracy was still at c. 70 per cent of the population in rural areas (Cressy, 1977: 9–10; 1980: 72).

For case studies of the likes above, practical literacy is often detected through evidence available from surviving signature material, the collection of which usually requires an in-depth understanding of standard vs. non-standard handwritten word spellings, a pragmatically informed knowledge of stylistic differences in historical evidence (e.g. politeness and power relationships underlying the various uses of punctuation and capitalisation), and a solid grasp of historical calligraphic styles.

As argued by Fox (2017: 136), sixteenth- and seventeenth-century handwriting in particular followed many different patterns and styles, from the very frequent "secretary hand", to the more "arcane legal styles" and even the more well-known "italic script" – all of which made reading an exceptionally challenging task. It is especially at this complex intersection that the work of an English writing system scholar usefully integrates that of a researcher involved in literacy studies.

Discussion Material

1. Can you think of any word examples where the length effect may not apply? If so, can you explain why?
2. Using some the references provided in section 8.1 to handbook and textbook material focused on text comprehension, explore in greater detail the orthographic processes involved in the construction of the surface level of text comprehension.
3. Using an excerpt from a text of your choice, identify the five parameters established by Zwaan et al. (1995) for the construction of the textbase (section 8.1), and reflect about how your own background knowledge affects the text's situational level.
4. Drawing on your past experience as a school student, can you recall any examples of ways in which writing as an element of literacy acquisition was treated prescriptively in teaching practice?
5. In what ways can signature-informed evidence help us to understand literacy today, when literacy levels are much higher and more equally distributed than those of sixteenth- and seventeenth-century England?

Recommendations for Reading

Berninger, Virginia W. (2014 [1994]), 'Codes, connections, context and constructive processes: Integrating the Vygotskian and Lurian perspectives', in Egbert M. H. Assink (ed.), *Literacy Acquisition and Social Context*, London and New York: Routledge, pp. 25–46.

Bus, Adriana G. (2014 [1994]), 'The role of social context in emergent literacy', in Egbert M. H. Assink (ed.), *Literacy Acquisition and Social Context*, London and New York: Routledge, pp. 9–24.

Gernsbacher, Morton A. and Michael P. Kaschak. (2013), 'Text comprehension', in Daniel Reisberg (ed.), *The Oxford Handbook of Cognitive Psychology*, Oxford: Oxford University Press, pp. 462–474.

Kintsch, Walter and Katherine A. Rawson (2005), 'Comprehension', in Margaret J. Snowling and Charles Hulme (eds), *The Science of Reading: A Handbook*, Oxford and Malden: Blackwell, pp. 209–226.

Molekamp, Femke (2006), 'Using a collection to discover reading practices: The British Library Geneva Bibles and a history of their early modern readers', *Electronic British Library Journal*, article 10, available at <http://www.bl.uk/eblj/2006articles/article10.html> [accessed February 2024].

9 Conclusion

This textbook has covered theoretical and practical aspects of the English writing system, providing a foundation of knowledge for those interested in studying the written realm of the English language. The early part of this textbook has provided background information about writing and speech as two different but complementary levels of communication, and has given an overview of writing system typology, in order to help students compare the characteristics of the English writing system with those of other writing systems from around the world.

Drawing on knowledge available in grapholinguistics, this textbook has established definitions for key terms such as *writing systems*, *orthography*, *spelling* and *script*, illustrating some of the limitations and possible overlaps existing in and across some of these labels. Definitions for key components of the English writing system, such as the *grapheme*, the *graph*, the *glyph*, *punctuation* and *capitalisation*, were also provided in this book. To my knowledge, this is the first time that a textbook on the English writing system focuses on establishing key definitions of the type explained above, dedicating considerable space to punctuation and capitalisation especially. Such an achievement has been made possible by recent advances not only in the field of grapholinguistics more broadly, but also in the study of English punctuation and capitalisation, both from a present-day and an historical perspective.

An additional, innovative aspect of this textbook has been that of discussing a number of case studies in which the English writing system is situated in interdisciplinary contexts, focusing especially on sociology, bibliography, the psychology of reading, and literacy studies. This is the first time in which detailed attention is paid, in a textbook of this kind, to each of the four areas of investigation mentioned above, in recognition of the advances made in and across these fields over the last few decades. While covering these and all the other areas of discussion mentioned above, this textbook has addressed issues inherent to the historical aspect of the English writing system in a creative way, by drawing on sixteenth- and seventeenth-century English spelling in particular as a fertile area of empirical interest, and embedding these discussions in broader theoretical, methodological and analytical discourses.

In many ways, the perspectives followed in this textbook have been fruitful, and it is hoped that the final product has allowed readers to learn key information about the English writing system which can be applied to other areas of their own linguistic and extra-linguistic training. However, this textbook also has some inevitable limitations. One of these limitations is the fact that the book reports knowledge on the topic attained up to the particular moment in time in which it is written. The theoretical information provided, in particular, is the fruit of grapholinguistic debates that are still in their early days, and which are likely to change, as they continue to unfold, the overall profile and complexity of the discipline over the next few decades. Future grapholinguistic knowledge is likely to be further enriched by non-Western linguistic perspectives, especially from languages which use non-alphabetic writing systems, and by new advances made in historical linguistics, sociolinguistics and artificial intelligence.

Another way in which this textbook is limited in the extent of information provided is in the fact that the insights provided in Part III reflect knowledge applicable mostly to areas in which I, as author of this textbook, have working experience. While these are clearly highly relevant areas of discussion in a textbook on the English writing system from my perspective, they are not to be considered as fully representative of all interdisciplinary areas in which the English writing system plays a major empirical role. Providing a serious, comprehensive overview of interdisciplinary areas that connect, even broadly, to the English writing system is a task that requires input from more than one individual writer; it could perhaps be the end goal of an international conference. Examples, however, include medical humanities and psychotherapy, where orthography may be studied as a means to detect patterns among writers and to help prevent or aid in detecting mental health issues; forensic studies, where writing samples may be used to identify individuals involved in a crime; and journalism and publishing, where the visual aspect of writing becomes just as important as its communicative content for marketing purposes.

Some of these areas are clearly likely to foster discussions on different practical applications of the English writing system than those discussed in this textbook, but they may also shift the focus onto different historical eras from those covered here. Corpus linguistics, for example, could offer insights into Old and Middle English, while forensic linguistics could allow perspectives into Late Modern English orthography.

Likewise, politics and culture might afford insights into contemporary issues in English orthography, while creative writing could usher in a discussion of case studies in nineteenth- and twentieth-century English. A broader perspective into empirical aspects of the English writing system may help future textbooks to also enrich the breadth of topics covered and to discuss in greater depth issues that were only mentioned briefly in this book. For example, future work could focus on aspects of teaching English as a foreign language, the influence of globalisation and international Englishes on English orthography, the relationship between cognitive and physical impairments and the English writing system, and many more.

While being limited, however, the present textbook is helpful not only with its unique approach to introducing the linguistic study of written English, but also for the outline it inevitably forms of the English writing system as an area of growing linguistic and interdisciplinary interest. Much like well-established areas of linguistic enquiry such as phonology, semantics, syntax and lexicography, English orthography appears to have a relatively solid theoretical foundation, which, albeit not perfect, allows scholars involved in studying the English writing system to establish meaningful dialogues and to understand each other. The methodological and empirical aspect of English orthography is undergoing impressive changes towards greater complexity, afforded by recent advances made in computer programming, digitisation, corpus development and artificial intelligence. These relatively new approaches to studying English orthography are helping scholars to detach themselves from old approaches based almost exclusively on using spelling as evidence for pronunciation issues, and to focus on orthography for its own sake. Whether questions arising from these new approaches to generating linguistic knowledge are likely to remain relevant for a long time or not, the growing popularity of the English writing system among students and scholars alike represents an additional reason to believe that the study of written English as an academic subject is here to stay. It is hoped that these thoughts will encourage many to make the most of textbooks like the present one.

Glossary

Acronym: short forms of earlier multi-word phrases or sentences, which usually retain the same meaning as the original multi-word forms from which they derive and which are pronounced as individual words (Brown, 2019: 102).

Allograph: a graphematic unit of analysis that expresses a non-contrastive linguistic function, and which signals an alternation that takes a grammatical, rather than a phonological function. On many occasions, the allograph does not change the meaning of a word in a meaningful way (Coulmas, 1996a: 173–174; Rogers, 2005: 10).

Alphabets: short for alphabetic writing system, it is a writing system primarily consisting of letters of the alphabet (Gnanadesikan, 2023: 41) (see *phonographic writing system*).

Any-spelling principle: a principle whereby written units can indicate meaning without representing sound in any consistent way at all (Ryan, 2018: 85).

Apostrophe: a punctuation mark generally used to indicate ownership and to signal an elision (*Oxford English Dictionary*, 'apostrophe').

Ascender: in typography this is the part of a letter that stretches above the x-height, such as the top portion of the physical letter *f* (Gaskell, 1972: 9).

Baseline: in typography this is the imaginary horizontal line on which all letters normally stand, and which usually corresponds to a line on a page (Gaskell, 1972: 9).

Bicapitalisation: words where capital letters are found in the middle of a word, originally formed by blending two individual word items (Brown, 2019: 100).

Bound grapheme: a grapheme that appears only in combination with another grapheme (Rogers, 2005: 11).

Capitalisation: the alternation between uppercase and lowercase letters in the Roman alphabet; it often marks the beginning of a sentence or draws attention to specific words within a sentence (Coulmas,

1996a: 532; Cook, 2004: 110–112; Hartmann and Szczepaniak, 2023: 70).

Character: a label sometimes used as a synonym of the grapheme or of spelling (Coulmas, 1996a: 72) (see *grapheme*, see *letter*, see *spelling*, see *symbol*).

Clitics: punctuation marks that appear attached to graphemes (Kirchhoff and Primus, 2016: 95).

Colon: a punctuation mark used to make an assertion that further qualifies a preceding sentence (*Oxford English Dictionary*, 'colon').

Comma: a punctuation mark generally used as a tool for enhancing semantic clarity; it is a solution for joining or splitting clauses (*Oxford English Dictionary*, 'comma').

Content words: words that have a meaning, including nouns, verbs and adjectives (Cook, 2004: 38, 56).

Cursive: a rounded writing style that started out as a series of letters formed individually and ended up becoming a series of rapidly written letters made with few (or even single) pen strokes (Sampson, 1985: 111).

Dash: a punctuation mark used to indicate a digression. Dashes are identifiable in two subtypes, the 'en' dash and the 'em' dash (*Oxford English Dictionary*, 'em dash', 'en dash').

Decoding: the process of reading, i.e. writing consumption (Condorelli, 2024: 3).

Deep orthography: writing systems that provide a more indirect relationship between sounds and spellings and therefore obscure our understanding of how individual words are pronounced on the basis of their written form (Rogers, 2005: 177; Tamošiūnaitė, 2023: 83–84).

Descender: in typography this is the section of a letter that stretches below the x-height, such as the lower portion of the physical letter *y* (Gaskell, 1972: 9).

Diacritics: graphic units that are added to individual letters as part of the overall orthographic form of an individual word (Coulmas, 1996a: 126–127).

Digraph: a two-letter grapheme indicating one sound (Rogers, 2005: 16, 292).

Diminuendo: a stylistic feature that, in historical English, affects the first line of a new text or chapter and consists of the use of a large-sized capital letter, immediately followed by a smaller letter, then an even smaller one, and so on, gradually reaching a lowercase letter size used by default for the majority of the text (Parkes, 1992 [2016]: 25, 34, 175).

Distinctiveness principle: a principle that indicates that individual words should be identifiable by their own unique spelling forms (Ryan, 2016: 55; 2018: 82).

Ellipsis: a punctuation mark that consists in the repetition of the full stop (normally totalling three dots) to indicate that a portion of text has been omitted, especially within square brackets (*Oxford English Dictionary*, 'ellipsis').

Encoding: the process of writing production (Condorelli, 2024: 3).

Exclamation mark: a punctuation mark used in order to indicate sentences in which the speaker/writer usually expresses emphasis (e.g. surprise or excitement) (*Oxford English Dictionary*, 'exclamation mark').

Fillers: punctuation marks that take their own independent space and normally connect linguistic units of the same category (Kirchhoff and Primus, 2016: 96).

Free allography: variation occurring irrespectively of the position of the uppercase and lowercase letters (Meletis and Dürscheid, 2022: 155).

Free grapheme: a grapheme that occurs without constraints on position and graphic context (Rogers, 2005: 11).

Full stop: a punctuation mark generally found at the end of a sentence; it may also be found next to a capitalised letter to signal a type of abbreviation called *initialism* or *acronym*. It is sometimes also known as the 'period' (*Oxford English Dictionary*, 'full stop', 'period').

Function words: words with a primarily grammatical function, such as prepositions (Cook, 2004: 38, 56).

Glyph: the different shapes that a punctuation mark or a letter can take when represented visually; when applied to spelling, the glyph signals different possible stylistic variations of a single letter of the alphabet (Hartmann and Szczepaniak, 2023: 65).

Graph: the physical realisation of each individual sign (Coulmas, 1996a: 173; Meletis and Dürscheid, 2022: 63).

Graphematics: an area of investigation concerned with a descriptive, linguistic level of writing system analysis. It deals with all theoretical information that can be extracted from the practical application of a writing system, its spelling and its orthography (Coulmas, 1996a: 176–177; Meletis and Dürscheid, 2022: 115; Barbarić, 2023: 130).

Grapheme: a written unit that indicates a phoneme (definition 1); the smallest contrastive element in a given writing system (definition 2). The term is sometimes used as a synonym of the letter, the character, the symbol and of spelling (Coulmas, 1996a: 174–175; Rogers,

2005: 10; Hartmann and Szczepaniak, 2023: 52) (see *character*, see *letter*, see *spelling*, see *symbol*).

Graphetics: an area of investigation concerned with the pragmatic aspect of the study of a writing system; it is, therefore, the knowledge area where elements related to English script as a physical entity (its alphabet and its uniqueness) are studied and described (Coulmas, 1996a: 177–178; Meletis and Dürscheid, 2022: 56).

Grapholinguistics: the linguistics of writing; a German-derived linguistic subdiscipline which focuses on the theoretical and material aspects of all writing systems (Neef, 2015: 711) (see *linguistics of writing*).

Graphotactics: principled limitations on how written elements organise themselves both in relation to each other and hierarchically within the English writing system, from the smallest to the largest linguistic segments (McCawley, 1994: 115; Meletis and Dürscheid, 2022: 148).

Historical orthography: a branch of historical linguistics focused on understanding the historical development of writing systems at different stages of standardisation from a theoretical, methodological and analytical perspective (Condorelli and Rutkowska, 2023: 3–4).

Homographic words: words where the spelling forms are the same but the sounds are different (Rogers, 2005: 16).

Homophonous words: words where pronunciations are the same but the spelling forms are different (Rogers, 2005: 16).

Hyphen: a punctuation mark normally used in order to merge together compound words (*Oxford English Dictionary*, 'hyphen').

Identity principle: a principle that indicates the fact that word spellings tend towards establishing visual regularity with other existing, related words in English vocabulary (Ryan, 2016: 53–54; 2018: 83).

Ideogram: symbolic graphic units used in order to refer to concepts in a relatively abstract way (Cook, 2004: 4).

Initialism: acronyms that are not pronounced as words; they are formed by capitalising the first letter of the words which one wants to abbreviate, followed by a full stop placed immediately after each first capitalised letter (Brown, 2019: 102).

Invariance principle: a principle that states that spellings have a tendency to crystallise in form (Ryan, 2016: 56; 2018: 86–87).

Length effect: a principle whereby words with a longer spelling form are generally recognised by the reader more slowly than words with a shorter spelling form (Yap and Rickard Liow, 2016: 456).

Letter: a label sometimes used as a synonym of the grapheme or of spelling (Coulmas, 1996a: 291–292; Rogers, 2005: 294) (see *character*, see *grapheme*, see *spelling*, see *symbol*).

Ligature: two graphemes appearing as visually, rather than functionally, joined (Rogers, 2005: 12).

Linguistics of writing: in this textbook, a literal translation of grapholinguistics (see *grapholinguistics*).

Logograph: a written symbol that has a strong linguistic connection to a word or a morpheme (Coulmas, 1996a: 309; Gnanadesikan, 2023: 32).

Logographic writing system: a writing system primarily consisting of logographs (Gnanadesikan, 2023: 32).

Lowercase: mostly in print, non-capitalised letters of the alphabet (Coulmas, 1996a: 532; Cook, 2004: 110–112) (see *minuscule*).

Majuscule: mostly in handwriting, capitalised letters of the alphabet (Coulmas, 1996a: 532; Cook, 2004: 110–112) (see *uppercase*).

Minuscule: mostly in handwriting, non-capitalised letters of the alphabet (Coulmas, 1996a: 532; Cook, 2004: 110–112) (see *lowercase*).

Morpheme: the smallest meaningful linguistic unit (Rogers, 2005: 295; Gnanadesikan, 2023: 32).

Orthographic depth: a way of identifying the extent to which pronunciation can be understood on the basis of the written form (Tamošiūnaitė, 2023: 83). The level of complexity in which an alphabetic writing system can convey sound-related information creates a distinction between deep and shallow orthographies (Rogers, 2005: 177, 295) (see *deep orthography*; see *shallow orthography*).

Orthography: this term sometimes has a polysemous value, as a synonym of 'writing system', 'spelling', or to indicate a branch in historical linguistics focused on writing systems. The term may also have a prescriptive meaning, indicating a set of rules aimed at regulating the ways in which the individual elements of the English writing system (punctuation, capitalisation, spelling) operate (Coulmas, 1996a: 379–380, 477; Condorelli, 2024: 2; *Oxford English Dictionary*, 'orthography') (see *historical orthography*; see *spelling*; see *writing system*).

Phoneme: the smallest distinctive unit of sound in a language that allows one to tell apart one word from another (Rogers, 2005: 296).

Phonograph: a unit in a given writing system that represents a sound or a combination of sounds in a given language (Rogers, 2005: 296; Gnanadesikan, 2023: 33).

Phonographic matching principle: a principle that states that word spellings are regulated on the basis of a connection between the written form and its pronunciation (Ryan, 2016: 54; 2018: 83).

Phonographic writing system: writing systems where there is usually a direct relationship between a graphic unit in a given writing system and an individual sound (Rogers, 2005: 296; Gnanadesikan, 2023: 33–34) (see *alphabets*).

Polyphone: a single grapheme that indicates two or more separate sounds pronounced consecutively as one unit (Rogers, 2005: 16).

Printing type: in typography, three-dimensional metal-based letters used in moveable type technology (Gaskell, 1972: 5, 9).

Punctuation: written signs used in order to structure written English and help the reader with understanding its meaning (Coulmas, 1996a: 421).

Question mark: a punctuation mark used in order to indicate sentences in which the speaker/writer expresses sentiments of doubt (*Oxford English Dictionary*, 'question mark').

Quotation marks: both single and double, they are punctuation marks used in pairs in order to report speech, to quote something from a different source, or to show that a word requires exceptional consideration (*Oxford English Dictionary*, 'quotation marks').

Round brackets: also called *parentheses*, these are punctuation marks used to provide details that are deemed peripheral to the overall meaning of the main sentence (*Oxford English Dictionary*, 'parentheses', 'round brackets').

Script: the pragmatic set of symbols used in a writing system of a given language (Coulmas, 1996a: 454).

Semicolon: a punctuation mark normally used to juxtapose two or more main clauses with closely related meanings (*Oxford English Dictionary*, 'semicolon').

Shallow orthography: writing systems where there is a direct one-to-one relationship between sounds and spellings; they are called shallow because the correlation between spelling and pronunciation is more explicit (Rogers, 2005: 177; Tamošiūnaitė, 2023: 83–84).

Spelling: the individual letters that form a word (Coulmas, 1996a: 477; Condorelli and Rutkowska, 2023: 3).

Syllabaries: writing systems made of syllabograms (Gnanadesikan, 2023: 33) (see *syllabogram*).

Syllabic acronym: abbreviations formed by taking the first syllable of each word in order to make a new spelling form (Jackson, 2002: 14; Brown, 2019: 103).

Syllabogram: a phonographic unit where there is an obvious correspondence with a syllable – either individual vowels or consonant-vowel combinations (Gnanadesikan, 2023: 33).

Symbol: a label sometimes used as a synonym of the grapheme or of spelling (Rogers, 2005: 298) (see *character*, see *grapheme*, see *letter*, see *spelling*).

Trigraph: three individual letters grouped together in order to signify one sound (Coulmas, 1996a: 512).

Typeface: in typography, the uniform stylistic layout of a set of characters used for printing. The term is sometimes used interchangeably with *font* (Gaskell, 1972: 16–33, 283–288).

Typology of writing systems: the theoretical organisation of writing systems according to their structural features (Coulmas, 1996b: 1380; Meletis and Dürscheid, 2022: 211–217).

Uppercase: mostly in print, capitalised letters of the alphabet (Coulmas, 1996a: 532; Cook, 2004: 110–112) (see *majuscule*).

Word division: also known as *word separation*, a process where individual words are split apart, most frequently at the end of a line (Coulmas, 1996a: 550–551).

Writing system: the overall visual apparatus used to write down a language (Coulmas, 1996a: 560).

x-height: in typography, the height of the physical letter *x*, taken as a reference point for measuring average character height (Gaskell, 1972: 9).

References

Abercrombie, David (1981 [1949]), 'What is in a "letter?"', in Piotr Ruszkiewicz (ed.), *Graphophonemics: A Book of Readings*, Katowice: Uniwersytet Śląski, pp. 9–19.

Albrow, Kenneth H. (1972), *The English Writing System: Notes Towards a Description*, London: Longman.

Anon (1939), 'Mr Chamberlain's last words', *Nottingham Evening Post.*

Anon (1969), 'MEN WALK ON MOON! TRIUMPH FOR MANKIND', *Milwaukee Sentinel.*

Anon (1988), 'Martin K. Speckter, Creator of Interrobang', *The New York Times*, <www.nytimes.com/1988/02/16/obituaries/martin-k-speckter-73-creator-of-interrobang.html> [accessed November 2024].

Anon, *A Quick Guide to Punctuation*, University of Lynchburg, Alton L. Wilmer Writing Center, <www.lynchburg.edu/academics/writing-center/wilmer-writing-center-online-writing-lab/grammar/a-quick-guide-to-punctuation/> [accessed January 2025].

Assink, Egbert M. H. (ed.) (2014 [1999]), *Literacy Acquisition and Social Context*, London and New York: Routledge.

Augustine, *Confessions: A New Translation by Sarah Ruden* [2017], New York: Modern Library.

Baayen, R. Harald, Richard Piepenbrock and Leon Gulikers (1995), *The CELEX Lexical Database* (CD-ROM), in Linguistic data consortium, Philadelphia. University of Pennsylvania.

Baker, Philip (1997), 'Developing ways of writing vernaculars: Problems and solutions in a historical perspective', in Andrée Tabouret-Keller, Robert B. Le Page, Penelope Gardner-Chloros and Gabrielle Varro (eds), *Vernacular Literacy: A Re-evaluation*, Oxford: Clarendon Press, pp. 93–141.

Baker, Philip (2007), *American and British English: Divided by a Common Language?* Cambridge: Cambridge University Press.

Baldick, Chris (2015), *The Oxford Dictionary of Literary Terms*, 4th edn, Oxford: Oxford University Press.

Barbarić, Vuk-Tadija (2023), 'Grapholinguistics', in Marco Condorelli and Hanna Rutkowska (eds), *The Cambridge Handbook of Historical Orthography*, Cambridge: Cambridge University Press, pp. 118–137.

Basu, Anupam (2016), '"Ill shapen sounds, and false orthography": A computational approach to Early English orthographic variation', in Laura Estill, Michael Ullyot and Diane Jackaki (eds), *New Technologies in Medieval and Renaissance Studies*, Tempe: Arizona Center for Medieval and Renaissance Studies and Iter, pp. 167–200.

BBC News (2013), *US Navy Ends Dependence on Capitalised Communications*, <https://www.bbc.co.uk/news/technology-22892166> [accessed December 2023].

Beauvillain, Céline (1996), 'The integration of morphological and whole-word form information during eye fixations on prefixed and suffixed words', *Journal of Memory and Language* 35, pp. 801–820.

Bennett, Jessica (2015), 'When Your Punctuation Says It All (!)', *The New York Times*, <https://www.nytimes.com/2015/03/01/style/when-your-punctuation-says-it-all.html>.

Berangar of Tour, *Rescripta contra Lanfrancum*, Wolfenbüttel, Herzog August Bibliothek, Weissenburg 101.

Berg, Kristian and Mark Aronoff (2017), 'Self-organization in the spelling of English suffixes: The emergence of culture out of anarchy', *Language* 93 (1), pp. 37–64.

Berg, Kristian and Mark Aronoff (2021), 'Is the English writing system phonographic or lexical/morphological? A new look at the spelling of stems', *Morphology* 31, pp. 315–328.

Berg, Kristian and Martin Evertz (2018), 'Graphematik – die Beziehung zwischen Sprache und Schrift', in Stefanie Dipper, Ralf Klabunde and Wiltrud Mihatsch (eds), *Linguistik – Eine Einführung (nicht nur) für Germanisten, Romanisten und Anglisten*, Berlin: Springer, pp. 187–195.

Berninger, Virginia W. (2014 [1994]), 'Codes, connections, context and constructive processes: Integrating the Vygotskian and Lurian perspectives', in Egbert M. H. Assink (ed.), *Literacy Acquisition and Social Context*, London and New York: Routledge, pp. 25–46.

Bible of Maudramnus, Amiens, Bibliothèque municipale, MSS 6, 7, 9, 11, 12, f. 4 v, accessible on <www.gallica.bnf.fr/ark:/12148/btv1b84521895/f14.item#> [accessed September 2023].

Bland, Mark (2010), *A Guide to Early Printed Books and Manuscripts*, London: Wiley-Blackwell.

Bloome, David and Judith Green (2015), 'The social and linguistic turns in studying language and literacy', in Jennifer Rowsell and Kate Pahl (eds), *The Routledge Handbook of Literacy Studies*, London and New York: Routledge, pp. 19–34.

Bloomfield, Leonard (1933), *Language*, New York: Henry Holt.

Bolinger, Dwight L. (1946), 'Visual morphemes', *Language* 22, pp. 333–340.

Boyes, Philip J., Philippa M. Steele and Natalia E. Astoreca (2021), 'Introduction: Writing practices in socio-cultural context', in Philip J. Boyes, Philippa M. Steele and Natalia E. Astoreca (eds), *The Social and Cultural Contexts of Historic Writing Practices*, Oxford and Philadelphia: Oxbow Books, pp. 1–18.

Bredel, Ursula (2008), *Die Interpunktion des Deutschen. Ein kompositionelles System zur Online-Steuerung des Lesens*, Tübingen: Niemeyer.

Bredel, Ursula (2011), *Interpunktion*, Heidelberg: Winter.

Brengelman, Fred H. (1980), 'Orthoepists, printers, and the rationalization of English spelling', *Journal of English and Germanic Philology* 79, pp. 332–354.

Brooks, Greg, Tom Gorman and Lesley Kendall (1993), *Spelling it Out: Spelling Abilities of 11–15 Year Olds*, Slough: NFER.

Brown, Adam (2019), *Understanding and Teaching English Spelling: A Strategic Guide*, New York: Routledge.

Brown, Gillian and George Yule (1983), *Teaching the Spoken Language: An Approach Based on the Analysis of Conversational English*, Cambridge: Cambridge University Press.

Brown, Thomas J. (2024), 'Punctuation in English since 1600', *Britannica*, <www.britannica.com/topic/punctuation/Punctuation-in-English-since-1600> [accessed November 2024].

Browne, George F. (1897), *Theodore and Wilfrith: Lectures Delivered in St. Paul's in December 1896*, London: Society for Promoting Christian Knowledge.

Bus, Adriana G. (2014 [1994]), 'The role of social context in emergent literacy', in Egbert M. H. Assink (ed.), *Literacy Acquisition and Social Context*, London and New York: Routledge, pp. 9–24.

Butler, Charles (1633), *The English Grammar [...]*, Oxford: William Turner.

Campbell, Ruth (1987), 'One or two lexicons for reading and writing words: Can misspellings shed any light?', *Philosophical Transactions of the Royal Society of London* B295, pp. 397–410.

Carney, Edward (1994), *A Survey of English Spelling*, London: Routledge.

Carter, Ronald and Michael McCarthy (2006), *Cambridge Grammar of English: A Comprehensive Guide to Spoken and Written Grammar and Usage*, Cambridge: Cambridge University Press.

Catach, Nina (2001), 'Graphetik/Graphetique', in Günter Holtus, Michael Metzeltin and Christian Schmitt (eds), *Lexikon der Romanistischen Linguistik (LRL): Band I/1 Geschichte des Faches Romanistik, Methodologie (Das Sprachsystem)*, Tubingen: Niemeyer, pp. 725–735.

Cathach of St Columba, MS 12 R 33, f. 4 r, Royal Irish Academy, <www.isos.dias.ie/RIA/RIA_MS_12_R_33.html#11> and <www.isos.dias.ie/RIA/RIA_MS_12_R_33.html#12> [accessed September 2023].

Chomsky, Carol (1970), 'Reading, writing and phonology', *Harvard Educational Review* 40, pp. 287–309.

Chomsky, Noam (1970), 'Phonology and reading', in Harry W. Levin and Joanna P. Williams (eds), *Basic Studies in Reading*, New York: Basic Books.

Chomsky, Noam and Morris Halle (1968), *The Sound Pattern of English*, New York: Harper and Row.

Condorelli, Marco (2021a), 'Positional spelling redistribution: Word-initial <u>/<v> and <i>/<j> in Early Modern English (1500–1700)', *English Language and Linguistics* 25 (4), pp. 799–823.

Condorelli, Marco (2021b), 'The standardisation of *i* and *y* in Early Modern English (1500–1700)', *English Studies* 102 (1), pp. 101–123.

Condorelli, Marco (2022), *Standardising English Spelling: The Role of Printing in Sixteenth and Seventeenth-Century Graphemic Developments*, Studies in English Language, Cambridge: Cambridge University Press.

Condorelli, Marco (2024), 'Orthography', *Reference Module in Social Sciences*, <https://doi.org/10.1016/B978-0-323-95504-1.00007-7> [accessed November 2024]. To appear in print in Coulmas, Florian (ed.), *International Encyclopedia of Language and Linguistics*, 3rd edn, Elsevier.

Condorelli, Marco and Hanna Rutkowska (2023), 'Historical orthography: Purposes, ambitions and boundaries', in Marco Condorelli and Hanna Rutkowska (eds), *The Cambridge Handbook of Historical Orthography*, Cambridge: Cambridge University Press, pp. 3–26.

Condorelli, Marco and Anja Voeste (2020), 'Synergic dialogue in historical orthography: National philologies, comparability and questions for the future', in Marco Condorelli (ed.), *Advances in Historical Orthography, 1500–1800*, Cambridge: Cambridge University Press.

Cook, Vivian (2004), *The English Writing System*, London: Edward Arnold. Additional topics and examples that integrate this textbook are available on the author's personal webpage, <www.viviancook.uk/EnglishSpellingSystem/SurnameRules.htm> [accessed February 2024].

Coulmas, Florian (1989), *Writing Systems of the World*, Oxford: Blackwell.

Coulmas, Florian (1996a), *The Blackwell Encyclopedia of Writing Systems*, Oxford: Blackwell.

Coulmas, Florian (1996b), 'Typology of writing systems', in Hartmut Gunther and Otto Ludwig (eds), *Schrift und Schriftlichkeit/Writing and its Use*, vol. 2, *1380–1387*, Handbooks of Linguistics and Communication Science 10.2, Berlin and Boston: De Gruyter.

Coulmas, Florian (2002), *Writing Systems: An Introduction to their Linguistic Analysis*, Cambridge: Cambridge University Press.

Coulmas, Florian (2013), *Writing and Society: An Introduction*, Cambridge: Cambridge University Press.

Court, Christopher (1996), 'The spread of the Brahmi script into Southeast Asia', in Peter T. Daniels and William Bright (eds), *The World's Writing Systems*, Oxford: Oxford University Press, pp. 445–449.

Court de Gébelin, Antoine (1775), *Monde Primitif [. . .]*, Paris: Boudet.

Cressy, David (1977), 'Levels of illiteracy in England, 1530–1730', *The Historical Journal* 20 (1), pp. 1–23.

Cressy, David (1980), *Literacy and the Social Order: Reading and Writing in Tudor and Stuard England*, Cambridge: Cambridge University Press.

Crowder, Robert G. and Richard K. Wagner (1992), *The Psychology of Reading: An Introduction*, 2nd edn, New York: Oxford University Press.

Crystal, David (2008), *Txtng: The Gr8 Db8*, Oxford: Oxford University Press.

Crystal, David (2012), *Spell it Out: The Singular Story of English Spelling*, London: St Martin's Press.

Crystal, David (2015), *Making a Point: The Pernickety Story of English Punctuation*, London: Profile Books [ebook].

Crystal, David (2019), *The Cambridge Encyclopedia of the English Language*, 3rd edn, Cambridge: Cambridge University Press.

Cubberley, Paul (1996), 'The Slavic alphabets', in Peter T. Daniels and William Bright (eds), *The World's Writing Systems*, Oxford: Oxford University Press, pp. 346–355.

Cummings, Donald W. (1988), *American English Spelling: An Informal Description*, Baltimore: Johns Hopkins University Press.

Cummins, Chris (2019), *Pragmatics*, Edinburgh: Edinburgh University Press.

Daines, Simon (1640), *Orthoepia Anglicana*, London: The Company of Stationers.

Daniels, Peter T. (2001), 'Writing systems', in Mark Aronoff and Janie Rees-Miller (eds), *The Handbook of Linguistics*, Oxford: Blackwell, pp. 43–80.

Daniels, Peter T. (2017), 'Writing systems', in Mark Aronoff and Janie Rees-Miller (eds), *The Handbook of Linguistics*, 2nd edn, Oxford and Malden: Wiley-Blackwell, pp. 75–94.

DeFrancis, John (1989), *Visible Speech: The Diverse Oneness of Writing Systems*, Honolulu: University of Hawaii Press.

Devitt, Amy (1989), *Standardising Written English: Diffusion in the Case of Scotland 1520–1659*, Cambridge: Cambridge University Press.

Dürscheid, Christa (2016 [1st edn 2002]), *Einführung in die Schriftlinguistik*, 5th edn, Göttingen: Vandenhoeck & Ruprecht.

Ehri, Linnea C. (2015), 'How children learn to read words', in Alexander Pollatsek and Rebecca Treiman (eds), *The Oxford Handbook of Reading*, Oxford: Oxford University Press, pp. 293–310.

Elfenbein, Andrew (2006), 'Cognitive science and the history of reading', *Publications of the Modern Language Association of America* 121 (2), pp. 484–502.

Elliott, Ralph W. V. (1963), *Runes: An Introduction*, Manchester: Manchester University Press.

Finnegan, Ruth (2024), *Communicating: The Multiple Modes of Human Communication*, 3rd edn, London and New York: Routledge.

Ford, Wyn (1993), 'The problem of literacy in Early Modern England', *History* 78 (252), pp. 22–37.

Fowler, Henry W. and Francis G. Fowler (1906), *The King's English*, Oxford: The Clarendon Press.

Fox, Adam (2017), 'Words, words, words: Education, literacy and print', in Keith Wrightson (ed.), *A Social History of England, 1500–1750*, Cambridge: Cambridge University Press, pp. 129–151.

Franklin, Benjamin (1789 [1891]), *To Noah Webster, On New-Fangled Modes of Writing and Printing*, in Edmund Stedman and Ellen M. Hutchinson (comps), *A Library of American Literature: An Anthology in Eleven Volumes* (1891), available on <www.bartleby.com/lit-hub/a-library-of-american-literature/1596-2/> [accessed February 2024].

Gaskell, Philip (1972), *A New Introduction to Bibliography*, Oxford: Oxford University Press.

Gelb, Ignace (1963), *A Study of Writing*, 2nd edn, Chicago: Chicago University Press.

Gernsbacher, Morton A. and Michael P. Kaschak (2013), 'Text comprehension', in Daniel Reisberg (ed.), *The Oxford Handbook of Cognitive Psychology*, Oxford: Oxford University Press, pp. 462–474.

Glassner, Jean-Jacques (2003), *The Invention of Cuneiform: Writing in Sumer*, translated and edited by Zainab Bahrani and Marc van de Mieroop, Baltimore and London: The John Hopkins University Press.

Gnanadesikan, Amalia (2017), 'Towards a typology of phonemic scripts', *Writing Systems Research* 9 (1), pp. 14–35.

Gnanadesikan, Amalia (2023), 'Classifying and comparing early writing systems', in Marco Condorelli and Hanna Rutkowska (eds), *The Cambridge Handbook of Historical Orthography*, Cambridge: Cambridge University Press, pp. 29–49.

González, Felix R. (1995), 'Spanish influence on English word-formation: The suffix -ista', *American Speech* 70 (4), pp. 421–429.

Görlach, Manfred (1990), 'The development of standard Englishes', in Manfred Görlach (ed.), *Studies in the History of the English Language*, Heidelberg: Winter, pp. 9–64. German version: Görlach, Manfred (1988), 'Sprachliche Standardisierungsprozesse im englischprachigen Bereich', in Ulrich Ammon, Klaus J. Mattheier and Peter H. Nelde (eds), *Sociolinguistica. Internationales Jahrbuch für Europäische Soziolinguistik*, 2, Tübingen: Niemeyer, pp. 131–185.

Görlach, Manfred (1991), *Introduction to Early Modern English*, revised edn, Cambridge: Cambridge University Press.

Greg, Walter W. (1966), *Collected Papers of Sir Walter W. Greg*, edited by James C. Maxwell, Oxford: Oxford University Press.

Günther, Hartmut (1988), *Schriftliche Sprache. Strukturen geschriebener Wörter und ihre Verarbeitung beim Lesen* (Konzepte der Sprach- und Literatur-wissenschaft 40), Tübingen: Niemeyer.

Hall, David D. (1996), *Cultures of Print: Essays in the History of the Book*, Amherst: University of Massachusetts Press.

Halliday, Michael A. K. (1989), *Spoken and Written Language*, 2nd edn, Oxford: Oxford University Press.

Hanna, Paul, Jean Hanna, Rrichard E. Hodges and Edwin H. Rudorf (1966), *Phoneme–Grapheme Correspondences as Cues to Spelling Improvement*, Washington: US Department of Health, Education and Welfare.

Hart, John (1551 [1955]), *The Opening of The Unreasonable Writing of our Inglish Toung*, in Bror Danielsson (1955), *John Hart's Works on English Orthography and Pronunciation* [1551. 1569. 1576], 2 vols, Stockholm: Almqvist & Wiksell, pp. 109–164.

Hartmann, Stefan and Renata Szczepaniak (2023), 'Elements of writing systems', in Marco Condorelli and Hanna Rutkowska (eds), *The Cambridge Handbook of Historical Orthography*, Cambridge: Cambridge University Press, pp. 50–73.

Haugen, Odd E. (2013), 'Dealing with glyphs and characters. Challenges in encoding medieval scripts', *Document numérique* 16 (3), pp. 97–111.

Hayes, John S. (1999), '1951: How can newspapers meet competition of radio and television?', *Nieman Reports*, <www.niemanreports.org/1951-how-can-newspapers-meet-competition-of-radio-and-television/> [accessed November 2024].

Hazen, Kirk (2015), *An Introduction to Language*, Oxford and Malden: Wiley-Blackwell.

Hazrat, Florence (2022), *An Admirable Point. A Brief History of the Exclamation Mark!* London: Profile Books.

Henderson, Leslie (1985), 'On the use of the term "grapheme"', *Language and Cognitive Processes* 1 (2), pp. 135–148.

Henderson, Leslie and Jackie Chard (1980), 'The reader's implicit knowledge of orthographic structure', in Uta Frith (ed.), *Cognitive Processes in Spelling*, London and New York: Academic Press, pp. 85–116.

Hernández-Campoy, Juan Manuel and Juan Camilo Conde Silvestre (eds) (2012), *The Handbook of Historical Sociolinguistics*, Oxford: Wiley Blackwell.

Hockett, Charles F. (1958), *A Course in Modern Linguistics*, New York: Macmillan.

Hopper, Paul J. and Elizabeth C. Traugott (1993), *Grammaticalization*, Cambridge Textbooks in Linguistics, Cambridge: Cambridge University Press.

Horobin, Simon (2013), *Does Spelling Matter?* Oxford: Oxford University Press.

Horobin, Simon (2018), *The English Language: A Very Short Introduction*, Oxford: Oxford University Press.

Horobin, Simon (2021), 'In our war of words, full stops are dying but the exclamation mark is doing fine', *The Guardian*, <www.theguardian.com/commentisfree/2021/dec/28/punctuation-complicated-full-stop-culture-war> [accessed November 2024].

Horobin, Simon (2025), *A History of English Spelling*, Edinburgh: Edinburgh University Press.

Hoskin, Philippa M., Sara Slinn and Christopher Webb (2001), *Reading the Past: Sixteenth and Seventeenth Century English Handwriting. Facsimilies, Transcripts & Reading Notes*, York: Borthwick Institute Publications.

Householder, Fred W. (1969), '*Language and its Structure: Some Fundamental Linguistic Concepts* by Ronald W. Langacker', *Language* 45 (4), pp. 886–897.

Houston, Keith (2013), *Shady Characters: The Secret Life of Punctuation, Symbols, & Other Typographical Marks*, New York and London: W W Norton & Co Inc.

Howard-Hill, Trevor (2006), 'Early modern printers and the standardization of English spelling', *The Modern Language Review* 101, pp. 16–29.

Hubbard, Eleanor (2015), 'Reading, writing and initialising: Female literacy in Early Modern London', *Journal of British Studies* 54 (3), 553–577.

Huxford, Laura, Colin Terrell and Lynette Bradley (1992), '"Invented spelling" and learning to read', in Chris M. Sterling and Cliff Robson (eds), *Psychology, Spelling and Education*, Clevedon: Multilingual Matters, pp. 159–167.

Jackson, Howard (2002), *Lexicography: An Introduction*, London: Routledge.

Jajdelska, Elspeth (2007), *Silent Reading and the Birth of the Narrator*, Toronto: University of Toronto Press.

Joyce, James (1916), *A Portrait of the Artist as a Young Man*, New York: B. W. Huebsch.

Joyce, James (1922), *Ulysses*, Paris: Shakespeare and Company.

Joyce, Terry (2023), 'Typologies of writing systems', in Marco Condorelli and Hanna Rutkowska (eds), *The Cambridge Handbook of Historical Orthography*, Cambridge: Cambridge University Press, pp. 138–159.

Joyce, Terry and Susanne Borgwaldt (2013), 'Typology of writing systems: Introduction', in Terry Joyce and Susanne Borgwaldt (eds), *Typology of Writing Systems*, Amsterdam and Philadelphia: John Benjamins, pp. 1–11.

Jucker, Andreas H. and Irma Taavitsainen (2013), *English Historical Pragmatics*, Edinburgh: Edinburgh University Press.

Katz, Leonard and Laurie B. Feldman (1983), 'Relation between pronunciation and recognition of printed words in deep and shallow orthographies', *Journal of Experimental Psychology: Learning, Memory and Cognition* 9 (1), pp. 157–166.

Kavanagh, James F. and Ignatius G. Mattingly (1974), *Language by Ear and by Eye – The Relationship between Speech and Reading*, Cambridge, MA: The MIT Press.

Kennedy, Alan (2018), *The Psychology of Reading*, Abingdon and New York: Routledge.

Kerl, Simon (1861), *A Comprehensive Grammar of the English Language*, New York: Ivison, Phinney, Blakeman & Co; Chicago: S. C. Griggs & Co.

Kintsch, Walter (1988), 'The role of knowledge in discourse comprehension: A construction-integration model', *Psychological Review* 95, pp. 163–182.

Kintsch, Walter and Katherine A. Rawson (2005), 'Comprehension', in Margaret J. Snowling and Charles Hulme (eds), *The Science of Reading: A Handbook*, Oxford and Malden: Blackwell, pp. 209–226.

Kirby, Jen (2018), 'The mystery behind Trump's Twitter capitalization habit, somewhat explained. An official proclamation from the Trump Manual of Style: It's "for emphasis"', *Vox*, <www.vox.com/2018/7/3/17532802/trump-capitalization-tweet> [accessed December 2024].

Kirchhoff, Frank and Beatrice Primus (2016), 'Punctuation', in Vivian Cook and Des Ryan (eds), *The Routledge Handbook of the English Writing System*, London and New York: Routledge, pp. 93–109.

Labov, William (1994), *Principles of Linguistic Change. Volume 1: Internal Factors*, Oxford: Blackwell.

Lass, Roger (1999), 'Phonology and morphology', in Roger Lass (ed.), *The Cambridge History of the English Language*, vol. 3, *1476–1776*, Cambridge: Cambridge University Press, pp. 56–186.

Leech, Geoffrey, Paul Rayson and Andrew Wilson (2001), *Word Frequencies in Written and Spoken English*, Harlow: Longman.

Leith, Dick (1997), *A Social History of English*, 2nd edn, London and New York: Routledge.

Lenivonitz, Alan (2018), 'Trump's bizarre understanding of Capitalization is surprisingly Strategic', *The Washington Post*, <www.washingtonpost.com/news/posteverything/wp/2018/05/23/trumps-bizarre-understanding-of-capitalization-is-surprisingly-strategic/> [accessed December 2023].

Liuzza, Roy M. (1996), 'Orthography and historical linguistics', *Journal of English Linguistics* 24 (1), pp. 25–44.

Logan, Conrad T. (1937), 'Noah Webster's influence on American spelling', *The Elementary English Review* 14 (1), pp. 18–21.

McCawley, James D. (1994), 'Some graphotactic constraints', in William C. Watt (ed.), *Writing Systems and Cognition* (Neuropsychology and Cognition 6), Dordrecht: Springer, pp. 115–127.

McColl Millar, Robert (2012), *English Historical Sociolinguistics*, Edinburgh: Edinburgh University Press.

McKnight, George H. (1968 [1928]), *The Evolution of the English Language*, New York: Dover.

McNamara, Danielle S. (2001), 'Reading both high-coherence and low-coherence texts: Effects of text sequence and prior knowledge', *Canadian Journal of Experimental Psychology* 55, pp. 51–62.

McNamara, Danielle S. and Walter Kintsch (1996), 'Learning from texts: Effects of prior knowledge and text coherence', *Discourse Processes* 22, pp. 247–288.

McNamara, Danielle S., Yasuhiro Ozuru and Randy G. Floyd (2011), 'Comprehension challenges in the fourth grade: The roles of text cohesion, text genre and readers' prior knowledge', *International Electronic Journal of Elementary Education* 4 (1), pp. 229–257.

McNamara, Danielle S., Eileen Kintsch, Nancy B. Songer and Walter Kintsch (1996), 'Are good texts always better? Interactions of text coherence, background knowledge, and levels of understanding in learning from text', *Cognition and Instruction* 14, pp. 1–43.

Meletis, Dimitrios (2020a), 'On being a grapholinguist', in Yannis Haralambous (ed.), *Grapholinguistics in the Twenty-First Century – 2020*, Part I, Brest: Fluxus Editions, pp. 125–141.

Meletis, Dimitrios (2020b), *The Nature of Writing. A Theory of Grapholinguistics*, Grapholinguistics and its Applications 3, Brest: Fluxus Editions.

Meletis, Dimitrios and Christa Dürscheid (2022), *Writing Systems and their Use: An Overview of Grapholinguistics*, Berlin and Boston, MA: De Gruyter Mouton.

Milroy, James and Lesley Milroy (2002), *Authority in Language: Investigating Standard English*, 3rd edn, London and New York: Routledge.

Minkova, Donka (2014), *A Historical Phonology of English*, Edinburgh: Edinburgh University Press.

Mitch, David (1992), *The Rise of Popular Literacy in Victorian England: The Influence of Private Choice and Public Policy*, Philadelphia: University of Pennsylvania Press.

Moats, Louisa (2000), *Speech to Print: Language Essentials for Teachers*, Baltimore: Paul H. Brookes.

Molekamp, Femke (2006), 'Using a collection to discover reading practices: The British Library Geneva Bibles and a history of their early modern readers', *Electronic British Library Journal*, article 10, available on <http://www.bl.uk/eblj/2006articles/article10.html> [accessed February 2024].

Mosley, James (2009), 'The technologies of printing', in Michael F. Suarez S. J. and Michael L. Turner (eds), *The Cambridge History of the Book in Britain*, vol. 5, *1695–1830*, Cambridge: Cambridge University Press, pp. 163–199.

Müller, Rudolf W. (1964), *Rhetorische und syntaktische Interpunktion. Untersuchungen zur Pausenbezeichnung im antiken Latein*, Tübingen: Eberhard-Karls-Universität Tübingen.

Murji, Karim, Sarah Neal and John Solomos (2021), 'Approaching sociology', in Karim Murji, Sarah Neal and John Solomos (eds), *An Introduction to Sociology*, London: SAGE, pp. 5–17.

Neef, Martin (2015) 'Writing systems as modular objects: Proposals for theory design in grapholinguistics', *Open Linguistics* 1, pp. 708–721.

Nellist, John G. (1992), *Understanding Telecommunications and Lightwave Systems: An Entry-Level Guide*, New York: IEEE Press.

Neuman, Yishai (2023), 'Analogy and extension', in Marco Condorelli and Hanna Rutkowska (eds), *The Cambridge Handbook of Historical Orthography*, Cambridge: Cambridge University Press, pp. 617–643.

Nevalainen, Terttu (2006), *An Introduction to Early Modern English*, Edinburgh: Edinburgh University Press.

Nevalainen, Terttu (2012), 'Variable focusing in English spelling between 1400 and 1600', in Susan Baddeley and Anja Voeste (eds), *Orthographies in Early Modern Europe*, Berlin and Boston, MA: De Gruyter Mouton, pp. 127–165.

Nicholson, Tom (2005), *Phonics Handbook*, Chichester: Whurr Publishers.

Nunberg, Geoffrey, Ted Briscoe and Rodney Huddleston (2002), 'Punctuation', in Rodney Huddleston and Geoffrey K. Pullum (eds), *The Cambridge Grammar of the English Language*, Cambridge: Cambridge University Press, pp. 1723–1764.

O'Reilly, Tenaha and Danielle S. McNamara (2007), 'Reversing the reverse cohesion effect: Good texts can be better for strategic, high-knowledge readers', *Discourse Processes* 43, pp. 121–152.

Oxford English Dictionary, Oxford University Press, <http://dictionary.oed.com/> [accessed February 2024].

Oxford Languages, Oxford University Press, <https://languages.oup.com/google-dictionary-en/> [accessed February 2024].

Papaconstantinou, Arietta (2012), 'Why did Coptic fail where Aramaic succeeded? Linguistic developments in Egypt and the Near East after the Arab conquest', in Alex Mullen and Patrick James (eds), *Multilingualism in the Graeco-Roman Worlds*, Cambridge: Cambridge University Press, pp. 58–76.

Parkes, Malcolm B. (1979), *English Cursive Book Hands, 1250–1500*, London: Routledge.

Parkes, Malcolm B. (1992), *Pause and Effect: An Introduction to the History of Punctuation in the West*, Aldershot: Ashgate [reprinted in 2016 by Routledge].

Perfetti, Charles A. (2007), 'Reading ability: Lexical quality to comprehension', *Scientific Studies of Reading* 11 (4), pp. 357–383.

Perfetti, Charles A. and Lesley Hart (2002), 'The lexical quality hypothesis', *Studies in Written Language and Literacy* 11, pp. 189–213.

Pollatsek, Alexander and Rebecca Treiman (eds) (2015), *The Oxford Handbook of Reading*, Oxford: Oxford University Press.

Price, Leah (2004), 'Reading: The state of the discipline', *Book History* 7, pp. 303–320.

Raymond, Joad (2011), 'Introduction: The origins of popular print culture', in Joad Raymond (ed.), *The Oxford History of Popular Print Culture*, vol. 1, *Cheap Print in Britain and in Ireland to 1660*, Oxford: Oxford University Press, pp. 1–14.

Reisberg, Daniel (ed.) (2013), *The Oxford Handbook of Cognitive Psychology*, Oxford: Oxford University Press.

Rogers, Henry (2005), *Writing Systems: A Linguistic Approach*, Malden and Oxford: Blackwell Publishing.

Rollings, Andrew G. (2004), *The Spelling Patterns of English*, Munich: Lincom Europa.

Rosen, Michael (2015), *Alphabetical: How Every Letter Tells a Story*, Berkeley: Counterpoint Press.

Rutkowska, Hanna (2012), 'Linguistic levels: Orthography', in Alexander Bergs and Laurel J. Brinton (eds), *English Historical Linguistics: An International Handbook*, vol. 1, Berlin: De Gruyter Mouton, pp. 224–237.

Rutkowska, Hanna (2013), *Orthographic System in Thirteen Editions of the 'Kalender of Sheperdes' (1506–1656)*, Frankfurt upon Main: Peter Lang.

Rutkowska, Hanna and Paul Rössler (2012), 'Orthographic variables', in Juan Manuel Hernández-Campoy and Juan Camilo Conde Silvestre (eds), *The Handbook of Historical Sociolinguistics*, Oxford: Wiley Blackwell, pp. 214–236.

Ryan, Des (2016), 'Linguists' descriptions of the English writing system', in Vivian Cook and Des Ryan (eds), *The Routledge Handbook of the English Writing System*, London: Routledge, pp. 41–64.

Ryan, Des (2018), *Principles of English Spelling Formation*, Trinity College Dublin, School of Linguistic Speech & Comm Sci, available on <http://hdl.handle.net/2262/82678> [accessed October 2023].

Saenger, Paul (1997), *Space Between Words. The Origins of Silent Reading*, Stanford: Stanford University Press.

Sairio, Anni and Minna Palander-Collin (2012), 'The reconstruction of prestige patterns in language history', in Juan Manuel Hernández-Campoy and Juan Camilo Conde Silvestre (eds), *The Handbook of Historical Sociolinguistics*, Oxford: Wiley Blackwell, pp. 626–638.

Salmon, Vivian (1999), 'Orthography and punctuation', in Roger Lass (ed.), *The Cambridge History of the English Language*, vol. 3, *1476–1776*, Cambridge: Cambridge University Press, pp. 13–55.

Sampson, Geoffrey (1985), *Writing Systems: A Linguistic Introduction*, Stanford: Stanford University Press [2nd edn published in 2015 in Sheffield/Bristol: Equinox].

Schloemann, Johan (2002), 'Entertainment and democratic distrust: The audience's attitudes towards oral and written oratory in classical Athens', in Ian Worthington and John M. Foley (eds), *Epea and Grammata. Oral and*

Written Communication in Ancient Greece, Leiden and Boston, MA: Brill, pp. 133–146.

Schwanenflugel, Paula J. and Nancy Flanagan Knapp (2016), *The Psychology of Reading: Theory and Applications*, New York: The Guilford Press.

Scragg, Donald G. (1974), *A History of English Spelling*, Manchester: Manchester University Press.

Sebba, Mark (2007), *Spelling and Society: The Culture and Politics of Orthography Around the World*, Cambridge: Cambridge University Press.

Seger, Benedikt T., Wienke Wannagat and Gerhild Nieding (2021), 'Children's surface, textbase, and situation model representations of written and illustrated written narrative text', *Reading and Writing* 34, pp. 1415–1440.

Shaw, David J. (2007), 'The book trade comes of age: The sixteenth century', in Simon Eliot and Jonathan Rose (eds), *A Companion to the History of the Book*, Oxford: Blackwell, pp. 220–231.

Snowling, Margaret J. and Charles Hulme (eds) (2005), *The Science of Reading: A Handbook*, Malden and Oxford: Blackwell Publishing.

Sönmez, Margaret J.-M. (2000), 'Perceived and real differences between men's and women's spelling in the early to mid-seventeenth century', in Dieter Kastovky and Arthur Mettinger (eds), *The History of English as a Social Context: A Contribution to Historical Sociolinguistics*, Berlin: Mouton de Gruyter, pp. 405–439.

Spector, Stephen (2017), *The Quotable Guide to Punctuation*, Oxford: Oxford University Press.

Sproat, Richard (2000), *A Computational Theory of Writing Systems*, Cambridge, MA: The MIT Press.

Sproat, Richard (2016), 'English among the writing systems of the world', in Vivian Cook and Des Ryan (eds), *The Routledge Handbook of the English Writing System*, London: Routledge, pp. 27–40.

Stubbs, Michael (1980), *Language and Literacy: The Sociolinguistics of Reading and Writing*, Boston, MA: Routledge and Kegan Paul.

Suddendorf, Thomas (2013), *The Gap: The Science of What Separates Us from Other Animals*, New York: Basic Books.

Tamošiūnaitė, Aurelija (2023), 'Orthographic conventionality', in Marco Condorelli and Hanna Rutkowska (eds), *The Cambridge Handbook of Historical Orthography*, Cambridge: Cambridge University Press, pp. 74–94.

Taylor, Isaac (1883), *The Alphabet: An Account of the Origin and Development of Letters*, 2 vols, London: Kegan, Paul, Trench.

The Bible and Holy Scriptures Contained in the Old and New Testament (1560), Geneva: Rowland Hall.

The Holy Bible [. . .] (1611), London: Robert Barker.

The National Archives (2023), *Palaeography: Reading Old Handwriting, 1500–1800, A Practical Online Tutorial*, developed in partnership with the School of Library, Archive, and Information Studies (SLAIS) at University College London, <www.nationalarchives.gov.uk/palaeography/default.htm> [accessed July 2025].

Toulmin, Stephen (1972), *Human Understanding*, vol. 1, Oxford: Clarendon Press.

Trousdale, Graeme (2010), *An Introduction to English Sociolinguistics*, Edinburgh: Edinburgh University Press.

Tyrkkö, Jukka (2017a), 'New methods of bringing image data into historical linguistics: A case study with medical writing 1500–1700', *Studia Neophilologica* 89 (1), pp. 90–108.

Tyrkkö, Jukka (2017b), 'Quantifying contrasts: A method of computational analysis of visual features on the early printed page', in Matti Peikola, Aleksi Mäkilähde, Mari-Lisa Varila, Hanna Salmi and Janne Skaffari (eds), *Verbal and Visual Communication in Early English Texts*, Turnhout: Brepols, pp. 95–112.

Upward, Christopher and George Davidson (2011), *The History of English Spelling*, Chichester: Wiley-Blackwell.

van den Bosch, Antal, Alain Content, Walter Daelemans and Beatrice de Gelder (1994), 'Measuring the complexity of writing systems', *Journal of Quantitative Linguistics* 1 (3), pp. 178–188.

van Vliet, Rietje (2007), 'Print and public in Europe: 1600–1800', in Simon Eliot and Jonathan Rose (eds), *A Companion to the History of the Book*, Oxford: Blackwell, pp. 247–258.

Venezky, Richard (1963), 'A computer program for deriving spelling to sound correlations', in Harry Levin (ed.), *A Basic Research Program on Reading*, Ithaca: Cornell University.

Venezky, Richard (1970), *The Structure of English Orthography*, The Hague: Mouton.

Venezky, Richard (1999), *The American Way of Spelling: The Structure and Origins of American English Orthography*, New York and London: Guilford Press.

Voeste, Anja (2007), 'Variability and professionalism as prerequisites of standardization', in Stephan Elspaß, Nils Langer, Joachim Scharloth and Wim Vandenbussche (eds), *Germanic Language Histories 'from Below' 1700–1200*, Berlin: Walter de Gruyter, pp. 295–308.

Werner, Sarah (2019), *Studying Early Printed Books, 1450–1800: A Practical Guide*, London: Wiley Blackwell.

Wharton, Jeremiah (1654), *The English-Grammar [...]*, London: William Du-Gard.

Wijk, Axel (1966), *Rules for Pronunciation for the English Language*, Oxford: Oxford University Press.

Wikipedia, *Capitalization*, <en.wikipedia.org/wiki/Capitalization> [accessed January 2025].

Wikipedia, *Capitalization in English*, <en.wikipedia.org/wiki/Capitalization_in_English> [accessed January 2025].

Wikipedia, *Capitonym*, <https://en.wikipedia.org/wiki/Capitonym> [accessed September 2025].

Wikipedia, *English Phrasal Verbs*, <https://en.wikipedia.org/wiki/English_phrasal_verbs> [accessed September 2025].

Wikipedia, *English Terms with Diacritical Marks*, <https://en.wikipedia.org/wiki/English_terms_with_diacritical_marks> [accessed September 2025].

Wikipedia, *Style Guides*, <https://en.wikipedia.org/wiki/MHRA_Style_Guide> [accessed September 2025].

Woolf, Virginia (1925), *Mrs Dalloway*, London: Hogarth Press.

Woolf, Virginia (1927), *To the Lighthouse*, London: Hogarth Press.

Yap, Melvin J. and Susan J. Rickard Liow (2016), 'Processing the written word', in Vivian Cook and Des Ryan (eds), *The Routledge Handbook of the English Writing System*, London: Routledge, pp. 453–469.

Zwaan, Rolf A., Mark C. Langston and Arthur C. Graesser (1995), 'The construction of situational models in narrative comprehension: An event-indexing model', *Psychological Science* 6, pp. 292–297.

Index